Feeling
GREAT

Doing
RIGHT

Hanging
TOUGH

FAVORITE TALKS FROM
ESPECIALLY FOR YOUTH

BOOKCRAFT
Salt Lake City, Utah

Library of Congress Catalog Card Number: 91-71406

ISBN 0-88494-797-1

First Printing, 1991

Printed in the United States of America

Appreciation is expressed to each of the contributors to this work. In addition to sharing their thoughts and testimonies with youth through the written word, these authors also spend many hours speaking to and directing activities for young people throughout the United States.

Contents

Feeling
GREAT

Doing
RIGHT

Hanging
TOUGH

1

Feeling Great, Doing Right, Hanging Tough, and in the Light

A. David Thomas

Our right to choose is the eternal refiner of our lives. If we choose the Lord's way, our lives are filled with light, joy, and a peaceful heart. If we choose the devil's and his path of darkness, our lives are filled with guilt, shame, and regret. Our loving Father in Heaven knows the impact of our choices, so he fills the mouths of his prophets with counsel on how to choose the right.

Lehi taught that the choice was clear—liberty or death (see 2 Nephi 2:27). Adam provided the right of choice by willfully choosing death so that man might be, live, and grow. The power is in us, God said, to "choose for [ourselves]" (Moses 3:17). Adam chose the right of choice for all of us, but it goes back further than that. Didn't one-third of the hosts of heaven choose to defy God? (See D&C 29:36.) Two-thirds, however, chose to come to the earth so that they might learn to know good from evil through experience and choice (Moses 5:10–11). Down through the generations, through his prophets God has pleaded with mankind to make the right choices. Moses asked, "Who is on the Lord's side?" (Exodus 32:26.) Joshua urged, "Choose you this day whom ye will serve" (Joshua 24:15). Hundreds of years later Elijah inquired, "How long halt ye between two opinions?" (1 Kings 18:21.) The choice is still the same today—the Lord's way or the way of the world.

Some time ago a dear friend of mine wrestled with the quandary of choice. He was just sixteen, and the world was pressing him for a decision. He lived in Wales, in a little community known as the Varteg, one of the few members of the Church who lived there. It appeared that he would follow the example of most of the sixteen-year-olds in the town and become a coal miner. In fact, he entered the mines as an apprentice.

Now, there is nothing wrong with coal mining if it is what you want to do and it makes you happy, but our sixteen-year-old friend was not happy. Every day he couldn't wait for his shift to finish. The thought of tons of rocks and earth above him chilled his heart. As he crawled like a mole through the shoulder-wide, chest-tall burrows in the dark, his soul screamed out in claustrophobic agony, "There must be something better than this."

Now, Father in Heaven knows how we feel and where we are. Even though it was under tons of coal, he could hear the heart of this sixteen-year-old coal miner. He spoke peace to his soul and told him that all would be well. The young miner believed that somehow God would help him find a way out.

Then it happened—an accident. It was a freak sort of thing, something that should not have happened. The coal and the useless dirt and rock were conveyed out of the mine in buckets attached to a frayed metal cable. One day our miner was leaving the mine when he stumbled. To keep himself from falling down, he reached out and grabbed the moving, ragged cable. Just as tightly as he grabbed the cable, the frayed, jagged metal of the cable grabbed him, and it dragged him along the ground. The cable tore his hand but would not let go. His blood dripped along the cable and trailed along the ground. He cried for help, but he was moving too fast. Soon the cable drew him to the opening of the mine, and then up off the ground into the air towards the waste dump of the pit. The weight of his body began to pull against the tortured flesh of his hand, and then it tore free. He fell several feet to the ground amid the rocks and was soon surrounded by concerned fellow miners.

Needless to say, he would not be mining for a while, and the quiet mending time gave him the solace to think. As he wandered the hills of Monmouthshire he sent the yearnings of his heart to God, his Father in Heaven. He told him how he hated the mines. He told of the jokes and stories of the miners—unseemly and crude. He told the Lord how dark and frightening it was and how desperate he was to get out and away. But what would he do? How would he make a living? At sixteen, most young men in Britain choose their life's work and apprentice themselves to it. What would he do?

Quietly but surely the answer came. He remembered that in school he had won awards and scholarships in the mechanical arts. His parents had wanted to help, but how could they afford to send their boy off to school in Birmingham, England? So the opportunities had been forgotten by everyone but the Lord. The plan, the direction, had always been there, but it required a disaster to make it visible. The young man's heart burned with the confirmation of a right decision. The Lord had given the direction for a way out. Would the young miner have the courage to choose the Lord's way?

He counseled with teachers, friends, and, of course, his parents. As with Nephi, the Lord told him how to build the ship of his life; it was up to him to get the tools and the resources (see 1 Nephi 17). There was a way, and more quickly than he had thought possible he found himself leaving his mountain home and heading for the plains of Warwickshire, his choice, and his future.

Our young miner's story is one of seeking counsel and of obedience. In Birmingham he found a struggle and sometimes doubt, but he got the needed schooling, subsequent opportunities, and finally the success he had dreamed of in the wet darkness of the mines. By continuing in the way of learning (see 1 Nephi 10:19) he sought answers, found solutions, and thrived. A wife, a family, and commitment to The Church of Jesus Christ of Latter-day Saints brought him face to face with one more choice: whether to remain in England with a secure job and future, or to risk it all and move to Salt Lake City.

I am sure you know the choice he made. As a result, instead of raising a family of disgruntled miners, he sired nine Americans—each pursuing his or her own version of the American dream—all because of one person's decision at age sixteen.

"How long halt ye between two opinions?" Will it be the world's way or the Lord's? Only you can decide. The need is for you to learn now how to bring the Lord into your life and then follow his counsel. His counsel and influence is available to us all, but how many of us listen and obey? He speaks through bishops and stake presidents, inspired youth leaders, and, yes, even your parents. He can talk through worthy friends, good books, and music. He speaks continually through the revered word of his scriptures. He can talk to us in the sunshine or in the star-filled dark. He can talk to us in the bustle of a public place or in the solitude of the bedroom. But do we hear and obey?

The Old Testament records a marvelous story about following through on good counsel. Benhadad, king of Syria, laid siege to Samaria in Israel. He brought in his armies, which surrounded the city and wouldn't let any food in. Food became unobtainable, and the people became very hungry. The head of a donkey sold for eighty pieces of silver. Mothers were boiling and eating their own children. And there seemed no way out of these intolerable conditions but surrender and death.

Now, outside the walls of Samaria there sat four lepers. The famine had literally sentenced them to a "fate worse than death," for not only were their bodies "falling apart" but also they were starving. As they sat talking together, they had an interesting idea. "Why sit here until we die?" (2 Kings 7:3.) They reasoned together that to enter the city would mean death by starvation, whereas if they went to the Syrian camp, where there was food, they might get some. And if the Syrians killed them — well, they would only die, and they were going to do that anyway. So they locked arms and marched to the Syrian camp.

Now, unbeknown to them, a prophet of the Lord, Elisha, had spoken. He had prophesied that on this day there would be an abundance of food in Samaria, but he didn't say how. Even as our unfortunate friends made their way to the camp of the enemy the words of Elisha were being realized. In fulfillment of his prophecy the Lord sent a noise. It was a noise as of an enormous army riding right into the Syrian camp. The Syrians heard it, and without any discussion they ran as hard as they could for the Syrian border. When the lepers arrived they found the camp empty, food still roasting over the fire, clothing and supplies in abundance. It was just as the prophet Elisha had said it would be. And because of their faith in an enlightened decision, they were the first to rejoice in the surplus. (See 2 Kings 6:24–29; 7:1–16.)

"Who is on the Lord's side?" "Why sit we here until we die?" "How long halt ye between two opinions?" Now is the time for each of us to choose. Liberty, life, peace, and joy eternal, if we choose the route our Father in Heaven has prepared; or death, oppressive guilt and shame, and the nagging spectre of regret if we take the lower, seductive path of the devil. It is our choice, our life, our eternity.

Now, I can hear you. You're saying: "O.K. God will hear and help Nephi, Moses, Joseph Smith, that miner in Wales. and four lepers in Samaria, but [and this is a good question] *"will he help and hear me?"*

And the answer is a firm "Yes!" if you will choose to live his way by being obedient and listen carefully to the whisper of His Spirit. "How do I do that?" O.K., I know you have another question — so perhaps you need another story.

I remember a young man who desired to have a real relationship with God. His own father had died and he needed a paternal influence in his life. He was sixteen, almost seventeen, and big as a man, but that didn't mean he wasn't lonely or afraid. You can be that size, have lots of friends and a mother who loves you, and still be lonely and afraid. He had heard all of his life about how God loved him, about how God understood, cared, and could help. He desired such a relationship.

He had been taught about being good. He had been baptized. He prayed every day, but he didn't feel he had the relationship he was looking for. So he sought to refine his life in an effort to make himself right with God so that they could talk. He was careful about his speech and the stories he listened to. He was even careful about who he hung around with. Certain movies and music didn't seem quite right anymore. He started reading the scriptures again. His prayers changed. They weren't a religious duty anymore or an exercise he did so that he could go to sleep without feeling uncomfortable. He really tried to talk to God. He felt he was making some real progress and decided to put a whole day, an extra day, aside for Heavenly Father. On this day he would be very careful not to crowd God out. He even decided to fast—not eat or drink for a whole day. He did it, but at the conclusion of his fast his answer, the response, had not come. He wanted to know whether God loved him, and he hadn't received an answer.

Teenagers can be such believers. This young man knew the trouble wasn't God—it must be him. Not enough time. Not enough faith. Not enough real intent in his desire. He decided to wait and, not thinking, he went to bed hungry.

The next day was Saturday—a special day for a teenager. He looked out of the window, and to his delight it had snowed. My friend was a skier and had a season pass to a local ski resort. Now he had no thought of breakfast or of his quest for his relationship with God—just six inches of new powder and a glorious, sun-filled day. He enjoyed a morning of skiing—excellent skiing.

Then it happened. In the tram on his way up for another run, he felt strange. He was sixteen and "cool," so he couldn't let on that he wasn't feeling right. Standing up, he locked his knees and leaned against the wall of the tram. The next thing he knew he was lying face down on the floor of the tram. He had fainted from lack of food. He crawled on all fours and sat up with his back against the wall. He realized he would have to make up his mind about what he wanted most. He could continue his day of perfect skiing—a glorious day, fresh powder (how many days like this would he have to ski?). The other option: his quest for closeness with his Heavenly Father. He felt he could only pursue one option—eat and ski, or continue in his quest to find God. And he knew he wanted God more than he wanted a good day of skiing.

As he rode the tram back down the mountain, he felt a rage building up in his heart. In his mind he yelled at God: What does it take? What do you want from me? At the bottom he opened the trunk of his car and took out a pair of shoes, since he couldn't drive with his ski boots on. He strapped his skis into the carrier on the roof of the car. He opened the car door and slid behind the wheel and started the engine. Then the rage hit again. "God, what do you want?" he yelled. "How much does it take to get you to speak to me?" In frustration, he slugged the dashboard helplessly. But as quickly as the rage arrived, it departed. He felt ashamed, and worried that somehow he had spoiled something or had failed an important test. He didn't know that God will often take you to the edge—to the extreme—to stretch you. But he never departs. He knows where the breaking point is. My young friend had not failed —far from it!

He bowed his head and pleaded with God not to give up on him. He asked the Lord to overlook his outburst, and he started to drive away. By force of habit he slipped a cassette into his car stereo as he pulled out of the parking lot. A quiet peacefulness settled over his soul. It was as if the outlet of his rage and the repentance that followed it had cleansed him, and nothing stood in his way. The road was clear, the mountains were dazzling with their new, pearl-white vestments. Below him the bowl of the valley was resplendent—a rainbow of color dancing in the clarity of a beautiful afternoon. He was overcome by the purity of it all. He pulled the car to the side of the road so that he could just look at it.

And then it happened. A gentle, warm flow of assurance moved over him. It started in his legs and moved up through his body, through his arms and his neck and head; a wonderful sense of "all is well," peace and control. It was then that his mind focused on the music and on the words of the cassette he had casually slipped into the stereo:

> All you've got to do is call,
> And I'll be there—
> You've got a friend.

The words of Carole King filled his heart and mind, and it seemed as if someone spoke to him. A voice inside him said: "My friend, that's how I feel about you. You can count on me. I love you. You are my son. *You can count on me!*" The sweet, gentle assurance remained with him. He turned off the stereo, looked at the magnificent view for a few more moments, and then pulled back onto the highway. He had received his answer. God knew where he was. He was loved. He had a relationship he could count on.

Only those who have talked with God know how he speaks. But the effect is like being in love. Remember—you'll know. And he'll help you find and tread the right path.

> There is a path that's firmly set
> That leads us safely home.
> But each of us must choose the course,
> Or we are doomed to roam.
>
> We willy-nilly choose our way
> And think it doesn't matter,
> Until we wake to find our life
> Confusion, junk, and clatter.
>
> It's simple to reroute ourselves
> And get back on the track,
> To turn, assess, and reprogram
> With a minimum of flack.
>
> Just drop your view down to your toes
> And see just where you're standing.
> Then assess just what's inside your heart
> And where you dream of landing.
>
> Then in your mind chart out the course
> Of where you have to go
> To get yourself back on the track
> And back into the flow.
>
> Now only one thing's left to do
> To get your future groovin',
> And that's for you to eye your path
> And start your feet to movin'.

God guides us in our choices by speaking to our hearts—our feelings—and our minds—our thoughts (see D&C 8:2). He assures us in our right choices by filling us with a powerful, even a burning, sense of confidence (see D&C 9:7-9). God is our guide, and Brigham Young made this promise: "If I do not know the will of my Father, and what He requires of me in a certain transaction, if I ask him to give me wisdom concerning any requirements in life, or in regard to my own course, or that of my friends, my family, my children, or those that I preside over, and get no answer from Him, and then do the very best that my judgment will teach me, He is bound to own and honor that transaction, and He will do so to all intents and purposes" (*Journal of Discourses*, 3:205).

Do you see? With God as our guide, all things work together for our good (see D&C 90:24). Our job is to seek guidance, listen carefully and obey, try to be good, trust that prompting that calls us to do right things (see D&C 11:12; Moroni 7:13-21).

And line upon line, precept upon precept, here a little, there a little, all will be revealed.

A. David Thomas, who holds a Ph.D. in Education, teaches in seminary, in youth and family programs at BYU, and in business classes in Salt Lake City at the University of Phoenix in Utah. His interests include reading, writing (his writings include a published book), running, and travel—"a trip to Egypt and the Holy Land is a treasured memory," he says. David and his wife, Paula, have six children.

2

Just Call Me Somebody— Nobody's Not My Name

Gary R. Nelson

Sometimes we feel that we don't get the respect we need or deserve. I have experienced that in my own life, which has been a series of downs and ups, ups and downs, and downs and downs.

Have you ever been picked on or felt abused? Have you ever wondered *why* God made you the way he did, or why you look, act, think, and respond in the way you do? Have you ever felt that life has dished you out a can of dogfood and dared you just to take one bite? There have been times in my life when situations assisted me to feel like a "Nobody," instead of like a "Somebody" as God intended. Let me share a few of those experiences and memories with you.

I can remember the time in sixth grade when I felt I had reached the big time. There you were considered Somebody if you were able to work in the school lunch room, right? You could have all the school lunch you wanted. (Now, that's a sad thought, isn't it? *All* the school lunch you wanted? Let's get real!) Well, all that was required for this job was to take down and put up the tables and benches. We even got out of school early to do it. What a sweet deal! We would lift a few milk crates around, too. It wasn't that big a chore for my friend Curtis and me. We were strong, growing boys. We could handle it.

Curtis and I had been the best of friends through elementary school together. We had taken guitar lessons from the same teacher, and basically just hung around together. He was "cool," so of course I thought I was cool, too! Until that day when I folded up the table and placed it inside of the wall and then forgot to use the wrench to lock the table into place. KAAAAABOOOOOOOOM! As I turned and walked away, it unfolded and smacked me right on the head, knocking me to the floor. Not only was the experience embarrassing for me and especially funny for Curtis, but it hurt both physically and emotionally. I somehow didn't enjoy doing school lunch duty anymore. It was no longer cool. I had failed, I thought. I felt like a Nobody.

Then there was the time when I threw my softball bat in a grade school softball game and knocked out one of my friend's front teeth. Or maybe the time when, during the course of signing yearbooks, we all took the "cool" and "in" way by signing our names over our pictures; and when I got my yearbook back in seventh grade I found that my friend Charlie had signed *his name* on *my picture!*

Or maybe we need to talk about my first musical solo in sacrament meeting. Sister Hein had bribed, persuaded, and encouraged me in this great musical feat for some three months. I was to be a part of a special ward Mother's Day program, singing the song "That Wonderful Mother of Mine." Can you just see it; can you hear it? I am an eighth grader. I am embarrassed as it is. What will my friends think? There I stand in front of the entire congregation, in fear and trembling, lyrics memorized, song rehearsed, and Mrs. Hein turns to me and says, "Be sure to look at your mother as you sing." Wrong! Tears flowed, I choked on my words, and just stood there for most of the song, a miserable failure. Afterwards my friends chided me. Of course, my mom was beaming and proud, but I felt just like a Nobody, a personal failure for the day. Playing the piano and guitar and singing are things I have enjoyed over the years, but that experience is still deep inside, and I have to come up with just that much more courage when I sing.

Or how about the time that I was chosen to be on the little-league all-star team as a first baseman? Just prior to the first game I went over to my scoutmaster's home for some last-minute training on the archery merit badge, and there I accidentally ran into an arrow that was lying on his couch. The bear razor hunting point went into my knee. It was a big enough gash to take away my chances of playing in the tourney against the all-stars from Kanab. Or how about the time in ninth grade when on the first day of school I found myself eating school lunch? By this time I had forgotten about the sixth grade prestigious lunch table job. I sat with all my friends. You know ninth graders — the supreme machines of the middle school, we who had arrived. We knew the ropes. We were cool. There I sat in my new Levi denim pants, my new cream-colored "Hang-Ten" tee-shirt, and my new black and white canvas converse tennis shoes. I sat chomping down on our fine meal of chili beans, creamed corn, cole-slaw, and green beans. Suddenly I heard a crash, then I saw a plate full of food coming my way. My entire shirt and pants were now a smorgasbord of food. I turned to find that one of my friends had tripped a seventh grade boy, and I was the beneficiary. Who needs a food fight in the lunch room when you can see food flying off trays? A fast trip home on my pedal bike and I was in clean clothes. A little late to my fifth hour seminary class, but I was not about to let a puny seventh grader make a Nobody out of me.

Or maybe we could talk about the time when, while I was a sophomore class president, during our homecoming activities our class bonfire was so hot that it burned a phone pole down; or the time when I accidentally let off the fire alarm at Boy's State at Logan; or the time when I forgot my tennis shoes on a high school tennis trip and found myself in Nephi, Utah, trying to locate a pair of 13-D shoes—an impossible task. Or how about the time in my high school senior year when my sights were set on making the all-area and all-state football teams, only to find after four games into the season that I had to have an operation to remove my appendix; I had been hit hard in a practice game, and my little appendix had been sent flying. The next day found me in the hospital less an appendix and out of football for four more games, with my high hopes of all-state honors dimmed. Or how about the time when I was playing defensive tackle on my high school team and I actually recovered the *sole* fumble of my football career, only to have the announcer announce the wrong guy and the wrong number, with no mention of my efforts. I had gone in and out of football history with the sound of one whistle.

Let's go back for a moment to my ninth grade year. That year did add more freedom. I decided to do without the threat of "mystery meals" in school lunch, so I joined my friends across the street at the local Judd's grocery store for a nutritious meal of barbecue potato chips, Twinkie, and pop. Sometimes, if we had a little extra cash, we'd slip around the corner to the Quality Bakery and sink our teeth into a nice fresh doughnut or a cinnamon roll. We would bring our snack lunches back to the school grounds and eat them under the shady trees. Well, you know, to be a Somebody you just did not eat school lunch.

One day during the first part of the year we were approached by an emotionally handicapped student—I'll call him Tom—to see if he could be a part of our group and could eat with us. He did not have much of a lunch. The administration had tried to mainstream him into regular classes and activities as much as possible. One of these activities was school lunch.

We knew that Tom would never be a part of our group. We wouldn't tolerate it. I mean, we were "Somebodies," right? I mean, what could he really offer to our group, being a Nobody? When he asked for a bite of our Twinkie we would say, "Sure." The Twinkie would then be ceremoniously smashed into the dirt by a foot or fist and handed to him. Tom would thrust the cake quickly into his mouth and gorge himself on the dirty, rocky, creamy contents. Loud and boisterous laughter was exchanged not only within our group but from the curious crowd. This ritual was repeated each day. How could anyone be as dumb as Tom?

Next he would ask for a swig of pop. This was also made available for immediate consumption, but not before dirt and grass blades were shoved down the bottle neck into the half-consumed contents and the bottle well shaken. Sometimes Tom would even down the pop in one full gulp or, with our prodding, drink down an entire carbonated beverage without a breath, suds and pop spewing like the volcano Kilauea all over his clothes. He enjoyed this acceptance and the manner in which we got our "jollies." He was our daily side-show, our very own Nobody comedy act.

The next year took me to high school, where I had been voted in as our new sophomore class president. The only reason that I can think of for my being considered for this office was my size. A junior or senior would think twice before he would dare push a six-foot-two 215-pound frame around. It worked. I did not have much hassle in the halls. It seems that in life you never really arrive at your comfort zone or safety zone. You are always in a state of progression towards that next level. Always wanting what is not; the grass is always greener at levels above you. The sophomores want to be seniors, the seniors want to be college freshmen, and the college freshmen want to be graduated and married. All along the way there is always somebody ahead of you.

On the second or third day of my sophomore year in school there was an opening assembly. There the cheerleaders led the sophomore, junior, and senior classes in a series of competitive school cheers. The losing two classes in this competition would have to come up and put a dollar into the blue and white spirit jug. The class that won the final competition at the end of the year would be eligible to keep all the money in the jug for their class.

Well, you can guess how miserably unorganized the sophomores sounded. We had never participated in such a competition before. The juniors were a little louder and more unified, the experience of one more year having made a difference. But the seniors were not about to let victory fall into any other hands. When the cheers were over, the head cheerleader asked both the sophomore and junior class presidents to come forward and put the dollar from each class into the spirit jug. Of all days not to have a spare buck, this was the day! The junior class president reached into his billfold and took out a dollar bill, rolled it up, and placed it inside the bottle. Luckily, a friend of mine came up on stage and handed me a dollar.

After slapping the dollar home in the jug, I proceeded to make my way off the stage. I hadn't taken more than a couple of steps when I found myself being pulled back onto the stage. The curtains were raised, and there I stood surrounded by a half-dozen jock-senior football players seated in their chairs. They were all dressed in their lettermen's jackets. Hanging down from the curtain behind them was a sign that read Jury. Next to them was seated another senior in black robes. He was "the Judge."

Then they proceeded to try me and *convict me of being a sophomore.* The idea was that if I was the one chosen by my sophomore class to lead them, I would be typical of *all* sophomores. So questions were directed at me. "Is he stupid?" cried the judge. "Yes," cried the jury. "Is he dumb?" yelled the judge. "Yes," cried the jury. "Then is he a sophomore?" exclaimed the judge. "Yes," cried the jury. The judge proclaimed, "Then he is guilty as charged!"

The crowd just loved it. It seemed as if the laughing and catcalling would never end. Up to that point in my life I had never been treated in that way. The humiliation was difficult to bear. There in that one brief moment in the midst of the loud taunts and jabs, I experienced the role of martyr. I was the insulted. I was the ridiculed, the victim, the scorned. For what seemed like an eternity I was transfixed.

Guess who I felt like? That's right, I felt like Tom. They say, "What goes around comes around!" Justice seemed to be meted out that day, but my soul cried out for mercy in the cage in which I was trapped. I began to realize what my abused friend, Tom, must have felt every day at our hands; the neglect, the ridicule, the inconsiderate, cutting remarks. My mind has recalled those scenes many times. Who was to blame for Tom's suffering? We had assisted in destroying a child of God with the weapons of thoughtlessness and selfishness, weapons against which he had no defense.

How awful it felt to be labeled *a sophomore Nobody* on that stage! How humiliated, how totally worthless and obstinate I felt! I wanted to evaporate. I wanted to strike back. But in a manly moment I held back my frustrations and tears until I could pierce my pillow in the confines of my own bedroom that evening. Terribly alone, shattered, tattered, and low, I still searched for acceptance. Sure, it was all in "fun" . . . but the scars remained.

Years of school leadership, college athletics, mission, and temple marriage followed. All proved to be vital areas of growth for me. About a year after my return from my mission, I found myself at a young-married age as a newly called elders quorum president. As I looked over my elder and prospective elder lists (a glance at a future stewardship), I came across a familiar name, one that I might have supposed time had erased. There was the name of Tom, the Nobody of ninth grade, the target of rips. The *Nobody* who was really a *Somebody!* He was one of the prospective elders in *my* quorum. He was then living with his parents. I had been called of my Heavenly Father to be his new elders quorum president. How could this be? What would I say to this abused soul of so long ago? How should I react? Could Tom possibly forgive me?

I knew deep inside what I must do. After much prayer and meditation, I asked him to come to my office. There we met for the first time in eight years. Both of us had experienced years of growth and challenges. The abuser and accuser now reached out his hand to the abused and accused. Those years had given me precious time to think, to reconcile differences, to learn and grow. I asked Tom if we might kneel together in prayer. I offered the words to that prayer. I pleaded with the Father that the right spirit might be present, that the proper words might be conveyed, that the wounds might be nursed and mended.

I brought to recall for Tom the hideous ninth grade days as I rehearsed to him the wicked, foolish, and selfish deeds of our group. I pleaded for forgiveness and asked him to please allow me to be free from the feelings of worthlessness and unworthiness that I felt for having helped destroy a child of God made and created in His image. While self-purging tears of sorrow streamed down my face, Tom simply said that he had forgotten all about those things and I was to please not worry about them anymore. We embraced. I have reflected often on this moment. Who indeed was the true Somebody? He had lifted me. If only I had grasped hold of the prophet Jacob's words in the Book of Mormon: ''Because some of you have obtained more abundantly than that of your brethren ye are lifted up in the pride of your hearts . . . and persecute your brethren because ye suppose that ye are better than they. . . . Do ye suppose that God justifieth you in this thing? Behold, I say unto you, Nay. But he condemneth you, and if ye persist in these things his judgments must speedily come unto you.'' (Jacob 2:13–14.)

In my years of instructing students in seminary and youth groups I have come across dozens of young people searching for an identity, youth who believed they were Nobodies. Somehow through the love of God and his Spirit they could feel that ''he denieth none that come unto him . . . and all are alike unto God'' (2

Nephi 26:33), that God would touch their lives through someone else, to help them believe that they were in fact a Somebody. In the words of the Lord to the prophet Samuel we read, "Look not on his countenance, or on the height of his stature . . . for the Lord seeth not as man seeth; for man looketh on the outward appearance, but the Lord looketh on the heart" (1 Samuel 16:7).

Such was the case with a student named Darrel. He was a sophomore at Roy High School, located near Ogden in northern Utah. Darrel needed and demanded a lot of attention. Like a puppy dog, he followed me everywhere I went. During lunch and before and after school, he appeared. He just wanted to be listened to, reckoned with, needed, accepted . . . loved! He had been told all of his nearly fifteen years of life that he was a Nobody, and he was believing this deceptive lie. Something within me whispered that he had a higher destiny. I felt that the only positive strokes he received all day came from me. I tried to take and make time for Darrel even though at times it was difficult. He so badly wanted to be accepted that he would do almost anything for attention or to be noticed in my class. He would offer to say the prayer, read the scriptures or the story, or volunteer to be the first to want to be a part of the object lesson or role-play experience. One day my class was in one of those "We're too cool to do anything spiritual today" moods. Darrel wanted to be involved. So I involved him. He ended up doing everything on the devotional! He led the music, said the prayer, read the scripture, and did the object lesson.

One day Darrel came up to me and said, "Guess what, Brother Nelson? Tomorrow is my fifteenth birthday! I just thought you'd like to know!" I had a pair of "sunshine officers" who were chosen as class officers. They anonymously went around doing things for people in the class; they would recognize birthdays and other special events in the lives of their classmates. I asked both Lori and Sheila to please put together a cake and a thoughtful card that we could give to Darrel the next day.

Bless their hearts, Sheila and Lori came through! But Darrel did not show up to class the next day. After some follow-up calls with the school I found out he had checked out of school and moved over to Clearfield that day. We could have dropped the opportunity to serve, but we did not—we felt impressed to find him. With Darrel's new address in hand and both class officers in the back of my car, we headed for Clearfield after school. We found that Darrel lived in a trailer court located in a poorer section of the city. As we entered the trailer park and started hitting the first of many speed-control bumps, there stood Darrel straddling his Sting Ray bicycle. The bike had no chain, and both tires were flat. He was having a good time just pushing it around. He shuffled over to us and said, "Brother

Nelson! You remembered my birthday. *You remembered my birthday!"* He motioned to have us follow him and led us to a shabby, aluminum-clad trailer.

He invited us inside to meet his parents. Lori and Sheila followed with the surprise chocolate cake and candles hidden behind their backs. His parents were gracious, yet backward in appearance and dress. Even though their vocabulary was simple, their manners were genuine and appreciative. "Mom and Dad," Darrel said, "this is Brother Nelson, my seminary teacher. He's come here along with Sheila and Lori to wish me a happy birthday." We withdrew from behind our backs the surprise cake and lit the fifteen candles. We sang him "Happy Birthday," and the parents joined in. It was a thrill to watch him blow all the candles out. Tears streamed down his face, and we too were touched by the spirit of this moment. As he choked back the tears, he motioned us to follow him out of the door. We said our goodbyes and walked down the trailerhouse steps. He threw his arms around my neck and exclaimed, "Thanks, Brother Nelson, for coming. You know, this is the *first* birthday cake I have ever received in my life. Thanks so much!" Tears filled our own eyes. He gave us his official bicycle escort out of the trailer court. We left spiritually lifted and subdued.

Each of us has felt like a Nobody at some time. We have all felt like failures. Whether it has been getting struck by a flying lunch table or forgetting our tennis shoes, we have all felt those feelings of discouragement that come with low self-esteem and lack of appreciation and attention. But *I can testify that each of you young people is somebody*, somebody really special. I love you, and I know that God loves you. You beloved youth, you were divinely created and should be divinely motivated to look at your differences in a positive and not a negative way. You possess greatness and have bright futures. In our quest for knowledge and understanding about ourselves, please always remember that you are somebody, and Nobody is not your name.

Gary R. Nelson, a seminary teacher in St. George, Utah, has been a seminary principal, travel coordinator, insurance agent, roller rink manager, motorcycle salesman, and taxi driver. He enjoys public speaking, writing, BYU athletics, singing, and all sports. He urges youth to "make the right choices" and "follow the Lord and his prophets." Gary and his wife, Christine, have six children.

3

Sacred Kiss

John P. Livingstone

I remember the summer that my mother met a missionary who had never kissed a girl. Never.

She must have talked about him every day for a month. "Kissing just gets you into bigger trouble. Just think of it—if you didn't get into the kissing, things wouldn't ever go further." It was scary. I could see an interrogation coming after every date.

She brought it up with my friends that came over. "What do you think about not kissing girls?" she would ask. "Tell me," she said, "do people get all turned on by hand-holding? A peck on the cheek?" The way Mom said "turned on" let us all know what she meant. My mom brought up concerns about morality the way other moms talked about the weather. It somehow seemed natural, yet caught you off guard. My friends really liked Mom, and her position on kissing became instantly famous—if you don't kiss, nothing worse would happen.

"Don't kiss the girls" she'd say. Oh, Mother, that's what they're *for!* I thought. She didn't go out with them. I did. And she didn't know whether or not I kissed them, and I was pretty sure she wouldn't call them up and ask them. At least, I didn't think so . . .

Well, Mom's famous kissing philosophy really didn't bother me all that much until the summer before my mission. Then I met Linda. She was normal. I mean *normal.* Other girls I had dated ranged all the way from airheads to pious, but Linda was normal. What-you-see-is-what-you-get. I liked her right away.

Some time before taking out Linda, I sat listening to President

David O. McKay during the priesthood session of general conference. Back in those days you went to the stake center and only *listened* to the priesthood session. There was no satellite transmission. A telephone connection was amplified over the PA system in the chapel. It could be fuzzy, like a long-distance call. President McKay was in his nineties. You had to listen closely, and it was easy to drift off and get thinking about other things.

However, something he said stuck in my mind and really seemed to hit me. He talked about a time many years before when one night he and a missionary companion had talked about girls. The companion told President McKay what his mother had said about love. She had said that when you find a girl who makes you want to be good, to rise almost above yourself and really want to do what is right, she is someone who is awakening true love in your heart. That thought went over and over in my mind. "She will make me want to be a better person."

The bishop had asked me to lead the music in priesthood meeting when I was about fourteen or so. I think I was the only boy in the whole stake who led music. That's what I was doing the very first day of early-morning seminary in my last year of high school. We were meeting in the chapel before separating into our new seminary classes. During the opening song I watched two girls come in the rear doors of the chapel. I was the first to notice them, as I was leading the music. It was obvious they were sisters. They were new and they were cute. One had dark hair and the other had lighter hair about the same color as mine. I've often thought that if the Spirit had tapped me on the shoulder and said, "Pssst, there's your wife!" I wonder what I would have said.

How about "Ah . . . I'm not married yet, Spirit!"

"No, dummy, the blonder one is yours. That is the one you're going to marry."

It would have been super wonderful to know then that the cute little light-haired Linda would be the girl I would take to the temple five years later. What a boost that would have been to my self-confidence then! But that's not how it works.

Well, Mother's kissing thing never really bothered me until I went out with Linda. When I was with her, I wanted to be good. I wanted her to think I was good. That is, I didn't just want her to imagine I was good. I really wanted to *be* good!

Suddenly, President McKay's counsel was real. She was the kind of girl that made me want to be a better person. It must be true love awakening in my heart! One night as I said my prayers, I asked the Lord if he could help me: if I had the strength to not kiss her on the lips before I left, could he make sure she was around and single when I got home from my mission? I am not sure the Lord makes deals like that, but I was earnest.

I can remember wondering how I could bring up the no-kissing thing without looking like a total nerd. I figured if I waited until some moment when I felt like kissing her, I probably would forget the counsel and just go ahead and kiss her!

I thought I'd better bring it up when we were driving. I had two reasons. One, driving down the road wouldn't be a "kissing" moment, and two, I wouldn't have to look in her eyes when I said it.

When the moment came, I asked in sort of a clumsy way, "What do you think about not kissing each other?" Even Linda knew about Mother's kissing philosophy. She responded, "I think it's great!"

The pressure that was relieved at that particular moment I shall remember forever. All we had to do was live the principle. That became tough. She had beautiful lips that seemed to cry to me, "Kiss us! Kiss us!" I thought that if I got really weak, I could just bite the car seat instead! It was a tough time for the car.

My deal with the Lord and my resisting the urge to kiss went super well until the night before I left for my mission. As I dropped her off, I kissed her right smack on the lips. Nothing more.

As I drove home I thought, "Way to go, jerko! You blew it!" I yelled at myself all the way. "Why did you go and do that!"

I remember we exchanged notes the next day at the airport, apologizing to each other. She knew nothing about my prayer and my deal.

As I climbed aboard the airplane and left into the mission field I felt some fear. I had been called to serve among the Navajo Indians and had to learn the language. Would I be able to speak Navajo? Would those people like me? Would I get along with my companions?

Now, girls, you need to know that any young man who serves the Lord with all his heart is going to think more about the Lord and less about you in the mission field. He will begin to get into missionary work in a major way and you are going to see his letters drop off a little. But that's O.K. Young men who learn to valiantly serve the Lord also learn the critical importance of a celestial type of marriage.

What a great experience it is to teach the gospel and touch hearts! The Spirit is the same in any language, anywhere. I found myself sitting on dirt floors in dirt houses called hogans. Most of the homes had no electricity or running water. We taught the people in the warmth of a fire by the light of flickering coal oil or kerosene lamps. We showed filmstrips from projectors powered by the battery in our pick-up truck. We bore powerful testimony in a language we at first struggled with, then learned to love.

I wrote faithfully for fifteen months; Linda wrote faithfully for eighteen. I fell in love with missionary work. She fell in love with another guy. Her last letter started "Dear John." Now, my name is John so her letter had included the quotation marks! She talked about how she had met him and was going to marry this good young man in the temple.

I sat and stared at the wall after reading her letter. Something really hurt down inside, but I only had about twenty minutes to think about it. We had a missionary discussion to teach that night and people to contact. I thought about that kiss Linda and I had shared the night before I left for the mission.

(Another thing, girls: I have seen "Dear John" letters posted on the bulletin boards of mission offices. Watch what you write. You don't know who is going to end up reading it. My letter stayed in a suitcase, but lots of others were mounted like trophies. Be careful what you write!)

Two weeks before coming home from my mission I received a typical mother-letter in the mail. Mother-letters are packed with information and every sheet is full, front and back. Up in a little corner of the last page was a note scribbled in the top right-hand corner. It simply said: "Linda is not wearing an engagement ring. I don't know why."

That little note seemed to sink into my mind a little more each day of the last two weeks. I worked hard every day and really didn't spend time thinking about what Mom had said, but it nevertheless seemed to hang in the back of my mind.

I flew home on a Saturday. It felt wonderful to have served an honorable mission. I was a real returned missionary. Me. Livingstone. An R.M.! Weird.

Mother and my "little" brother (who now weighed three times my weight and was solid muscle from being a brick-layer's helper) finally met me at the airport. They were half an hour late. They had gone to the wrong airport. I remember imagining the homecoming crowd. A band. Dancing girls.

Forget it! I searched the crowd of faces as I walked into the terminal trying to look as impressive as possible. I did not want to appear frantic as I realized there was no one there to meet me. I kept searching faces as I retrieved suitcases from the carousel.

I had felt pretty confident as the plane had touched down. I had loved my mission. Learned the language fairly well. Served as a leader. A district leader. An assistant to the mission president. Feelings of pride bordering on arrogance had started to creep in. Waiting that extra half hour was the best thing that could have happened to me. By the time Mom and Mike showed up, I was a humble servant of the Lord feeling lost and alone and without a companion.

Returned missionaries are heavy-duty. They play for keeps, girls. It's scary. When they look at you, it's different. Different for them. Different for you. Dangerous for your young single adulthood!

The following Tuesday there was a program and dance at the institute building. It was to be my first social outing, and I was scared. No white shirt. No tie. No companion. What will dancing be like? Maybe I'll just watch.

Friends had said Linda would be there for sure. She was in the program. Would I recognize her? Was her hair different? Someone had said on Sunday that she had new glasses. A look-alike walked into the room and I wondered if that could possibly be her. Surely I wouldn't have trouble recognizing her! Would I?

Then she walked in. My heart was in my mouth, but after two years of missionary work I knew how to maintain that dignified, aloof look. The program was fun, but when the dance started, things got uncomfortable. My forehead was in a cool sweat.

Another girl I had known before my mission came up and asked the question returned missionaries hate. "How was your mission?" she said. Now, that question calls for you to take two years of the most intense, wonderful period of your life—about ten percent of time since birth—and condense it into ten words or less. A sensational understatement is about to follow.

I stood in the blaring dance music and tried to look cool and answer that brainless question. Suddenly she said, "Let's dance!" My arm was grabbed and we were on our way onto the dance floor. Two years of missionary work and no dancing meant a weird wiggle from me, and the forehead sweat was no longer cool. It felt funny to be out there trying to dance. I felt lost. I felt undignified. I felt foolish. A fish out of water. Balloon out of air.

After that first dance, while I was still feeling a little defiled, Linda walked up to me. We talked. No brainless question. It was easy. Everything seemed natural. Lights did not flash and trumpets did not sound, but it was just nice. Real nice.

I did not have the courage to ask about her engagement or disengagement, but the next day something happened that I would have paid money to arrange. I wanted to meet the guy she had wanted to marry at one time. He was still around, and I guess the curiosity of meeting whomever had so completely caught her attention was gnawing at me.

University lectures began the next day, and feeling green and new all over again I started my second year. Registering for a class at the LDS insitute of religion where the dance had been held the night before was on my agenda. As I walked in that day I could feel the warmth of the Spirit there and knew the peace and refuge the institute provides from the world. I lined up behind another young man to register for a religion class. He gave his name to the secretary, and suddenly I realized I was standing there with the guy I had been looking forward to meeting.

It somehow gave me a surge of great confidence to know who he was without his knowing who I was. I knew that he would know my name well. And I felt that I had a certain upper hand in holding back my identity.

We joked and visited in line. Clever wit passed back and forth. I could tell he thought I was sharp. Our little visit came to an end when we had both moved through the last of the booths set up to take care of all aspects of institute registration. Just as we shook hands before parting, he asked my name. The look on his face was one of those a Hollywood director tries to encourage when the essential truth, the plot thickener, is finally revealed. He had been had, and he knew it. How sweet the moment! Once in a lifetime a chance like that comes along. My time had come.

It was two months before I had the courage to ask Linda to go out with me. I guess part of the problem was that I knew that if we went out, my single adult status would be history. And that was the way it was.

Once again, we had the little discussion about not kissing each other on the lips. I knew that if we could make that commitment, we would be worthy, really worthy, to go to the temple to be married. I was not going to make the same mistake again.

When we finally knelt at the altar in the temple, we were clean. The temple was beautiful. You cannot be married in a more beautiful place with a more beautiful feeling than in the temple. The altar has a deeply cushioned top that your elbows rest on. Your knees sink into a soft, comfortable padding. The two large wall mirrors reflect images of the two of you that seem to go on forever, unflawed. As we held hands and finally leaned across the altar to kiss each other as husband and wife, we realized we were sealed for all time and eternity if we would just keep the covenants we had made with the Lord. That kiss on the lips was the first since being home from my mission. What a moment! I wondered if it was O.K. to feel that way in the temple. The feeling was not one of lust or improper desire, but one of deep feeling, almost a reverence for this beautiful, wonderful woman who had just become my eternal companion.

Nine months after my coming home from my mission, we were married. Nine months (and two weeks!) after that we had our first daughter. Twelve months after that we had our second daughter. Fifteen months after that we had our third daughter. Nineteen months after that we had our first boy. Twenty-one months later we had another little girl. Twenty-five months later we had another little girl. Eighteen months later we had another little girl. Can you see how quickly life moves on? Have you noticed for yourself how time is picking up and speeding along in your own life these days?

Now, I am not trying to preach that everyone should stop kissing and that any kissing is sinful. What I am saying is that we need to set standards that we know, if kept, will keep us clean and worthy to enter the house of the Lord. Observing the standard Linda and I set was the hardest thing I had ever done. Yet it continues to bring a wonderful happiness to know that we went to the temple worthy and ready. That act of seeming sacrifice has resulted in a great blessing in our physical and spiritual relationship in marriage. Sacrifice now characterizes our relationship, and that relationship just keeps getting better and better.

I testify to you that when we put principles of righteousness ahead of our own carnal desires the Lord can bless our relationships. The sacrifice is so very much ''worth it''! The hymn ''Praise to the Man'' says that ''sacrifice brings forth the blessings of heaven.'' How true! Our love is not only still there, but also it continues to burn brighter, truer, deeper. I sometimes wish that we could take our feelings and put them into others for a few minutes just to let them feel what it can be like. ''There, now, doesn't that feel good?'' I would say. But that's not the way it works, and each of us has to make his own way through this wonderful life and earn the feelings for himself.

It is my humble prayer that you will resolve to set a higher personal standard for yourself after you have read this. Determine for yourself what your personal dating standard will be. Think about any current dating relationship you may be in. Does he or she make you feel like being good; becoming a better person? Are you inspired to do what is right in that person's presence? If not, have the spiritual courage to choose the right and get out of that situation now. Yes, it will be painful for a while, but the Lord will strengthen you. Do it.

I am so grateful for the principle of repentance that allows us to deal with our weaknesses. All of us have weaknesses. Yet the Lord says: "If men come unto me I will show unto them their weakness. I give unto men weakness that they may be humble; and my grace is sufficient for all men that humble themselves before me; for if they humble themselves before me, and have faith in me, then will I make weak things become strong unto them (Ether 12:27).

Thus the Lord gives us the formula for making our weakness a strength. Come unto him and be humble and faithful. Going to the bishop is being humble. Trying a new approach to one's problem is exercising faith. That we can do just that is my prayer for you and me, in the name of Jesus Christ, amen.

John P. Livingstone, a former CES coordinator, holds a Ph.D. in Counseling and is an institute director in Calgary, Alberta, Canada. He enjoys guitar and banjo playing, auto mechanics, computers, traveling, and country/folk music. He perceives today's LDS youth as "vibrant, strong, curious, and talented." John and his wife, Linda, have seven children.

4

But If Not . . . Three Words That Eliminate Compromise

Kathryn S. Smith

In struggling through medical school a young friend of mine had some bad days. You know the kind: the tests had all the wrong questions on them; he felt he was the only one who didn't get what the doctors were trying to teach him; his girlfriend decided to go on a mission just as he was planning to propose. I got a phone call late one evening. "Kathy, I just don't understand. I go to church; I read my scriptures; I pay my tithing; I am trying to be good! Why won't Satan just leave me alone?"

I smiled inside, thinking that possibly those right choices might have something to do with it. "You need a blessing," I suggested, and recommended that he seek one. He confided to me later what had happened when he went to the Lord for understanding. As a priesthood leader laid his hands on my friend's head, he learned at least part of why he was being tried so continuously: "In the war in heaven you fought on the front lines with the archangel Michael against the forces of Satan, and you did not give an inch. He wants you now!" My friend came out of that blessing with his chest about four inches thicker. "Just come on," he challenged, again ready for the fight.

There were only two teams in the premortal life, and there is no question which one we were on. Where do you think *we* were during that war in heaven? Can you picture yourself sitting back behind those front-line contenders, munching on a bag of popcorn and sipping a can of Sprite, cheering enthusiastically: "Hey, go for it, up there! You're doing a great job!'' I am sure that we, too, fought on "the front lines" with the forces of Michael, and Satan remembers you and he remembers me. He wants *us* now, and he will stop at nothing to distract you from the purpose you came here to earth to accomplish. It helps to be reminded what team we are on, but still we must demonstrate it with every decision we make every day.

My first off-campus youth conference was in Abilene, Texas. The stake president met us at the airport, dressed in jeans and a western shirt and wearing a bolo tie and boots. He stuck his hand out and with an infectious grin said, "Hah, Ah'm Benny, and this is mah wife, Ginger!'' He had his arm affectionately around his beaming wife, and we knew this conference was going to be fun. This wonderful stake leader had organized a youth conference for his fifty youth. Once a year he brought them together, and they came one from a town, one from a high school, in a stake having a four-hundred-mile circumference. There was a rare unity among those young people, and all of us felt it.

As the conference wore on, one young man particularly caught my attention. He was fifteen, blond and refreshingly handsome. Whenever someone seemed to be shyly standing apart, Jayson would go over to him or her and say, "Why don't you come sit at my table?'' "Would you like to go to class with me?'' "Why don't you come be on our team?'' I wondered if this young man was on the payroll.

The first night at the dance was no different. The youth were mixing happily, but there were still a few shyer ones on the outskirts of the cultural hall, and I was making the rounds, trying to get them involved. One young lady was standing alone, and perhaps she did not feel as pretty as she would have liked to feel. Perhaps she was not as slim as she wished; perhaps her hair was not as stylish as some of the other girls'. I was talking to her when I felt an arm slip around my shoulders and I looked into the clear blue eyes of this fifteen-year-old Jayson. "Kayathee" he began, with a delicious Texas drawl, "You're just gonna have to do without this young lady for a while because I want to dance with her.'' And he led her onto the dance floor. He could have danced with her and brought her back to me and felt he had done his part, but Jayson understood more than that. After he had danced with her he got his brother Jeremy to do so, and while Jeremy was dancing he got his other friends to ask her. Without her knowing he had done it, he kept her out there dancing the entire evening. I watched it all and thought, "This young man knows which team he is on.''

The last moments of our youth conferences are spent in a testimony meeting, and in this one Jayson ran up to the front and grabbed the sides of the pulpit. He and his family had moved to California a year earlier, and the boys had now flown back to Abilene to have youth conference with their friends. "California is a big place," he said, "I didn't know what to do with myself." He told us he had felt a little lost until Christmastime, when the ward had organized the youth to gather food donations for a Cambodian branch in his Walnut Creek Stake. They took the sacks of food out to the branch, and Jayson said that felt good, but he looked around at all the little children and wondered what kind of Christmas they were going to have.

He and a friend of his took the ward list and divided it between them. They called the members and asked if they would donate toys that their children didn't use anymore, rummage-sale-type toys, and bring them to the ward party that Friday. Jayson went to the party hoping people had remembered, and peeked up on the stage to see if there was anything there. The stage was mounded with toys, and most of them weren't used at all. The families had made this their family Christmas project, and there were beautiful new toys waiting to be wrapped.

Jayson and his friends literally stayed up all night wrapping the presents, and someone found a big Santa sack to stuff them in and a funny Santa suit to stuff him in. He was a long tall drink of water, so they found pillows to make him look chubby and fat. The morning after Christmas the youth piled into a car and drove out to the Cambodian branch. Those children came running like chickens for the morning corn. Jayson passed out the toys and chuckled his "ho ho's," and the air was filled with excitement and laughter. Soon it was over and everyone felt warm inside.

Jayson felt a little tug on his Santa suit. He looked down into deep brown eyes and heard a little voice ask, "Does Santa Claus have anything in his sack for me?" Jayson knew it was empty. He did not know why this little boy had missed the earlier festivities, but he swept him up in his arm and whispered in his ear. "Yeah, Santa had me save something special for you!" This incredible young man reached down and took off the watch his father had given him for Christmas the day before. He put it into this little Cambodian boy's hand.

Jayson looked out at us, his Abilene friends, and with tears glistening on his cheeks, he said, "I love the gospel of Jesus Christ." This young man knows what team he is on. In every decision every day he shows it.

My family moved to Provo, Utah, this past year, and my teenagers felt nervous to enter new schools. My twelve-year-old was particularly lost at first, and her face wore the signs of that. "How are you doing, Becca?'' I would ask her. She would shake her head. ''What are you going to do, honey?'' ''I guess I'm just going to feel like this until I don't feel like this anymore!'' Every night I would see her on her knees, and I suspected part of what she might be asking.

Then came the 1989 BYU football season. We went to the first game, and Becca scanned the faces of the football players on the Cougar program. She had decided to get a crush on one of them, and needed to know what they looked like in order to make her decision. She made her choice, went home, and took out a piece of paper. ''Dear Ty,'' she began writing in pencil. ''I think you're so handsome I drooled all over your picture.'' (I did not know she had written any of this until later.) She went on. ''My Mom says you are too busy to come and visit me, so I will understand if you don't come, but I would sure like to meet you.'' She signed her name, gave no map or address except what was on the envelope, and asked me if I knew this football player's address. Ty Detmer. I shook my head, but I knew that it couldn't hurt to mail a fan letter and I simply addressed it care of Brigham Young University. I did not think about it again.

Five days later Rebecca and I returned from the grocery store after school and noticed an unfamiliar Blazer in the driveway. Becca bounded into the house to get some help with the groceries, but no one came back out. I plodded into the house, arms full, and a tongue ready to scold children who ''made me do everything!'' I saw my daughter sitting on the couch in the living room. Her jaw was dropped on her chest, as if dislocated, and she was staring straight ahead at a tall, thin young man standing in the middle of the room. I entered. ''Hi, Ah'm Tah,'' he said as he stuck out his hand for me to shake. I couldn't believe it. He had stopped three times to get directions to our address, and had waited forty-five minutes for us to return from the store. He smiled indulgently at the little girl who was immobile at his visit. ''She sounded like quite a fan. I thought I ought to drop by.'' He smiled shyly. ''I have a little sister, and I think I know how she feels.''

Ty stayed and talked to my daughter for half an hour, allowed all the children in the cul de sac to come in and get his autograph, and then offered to go outside and throw the ball to them for a while. The children had a nerf football with stuffing oozing out of it and a soccer ball duct-taped together in several places. He patiently stood and threw those makeshift balls with these little ones for another thirty minutes. I watched him and thought that in every decision, every day, Ty Detmer demonstrates that he has more than a fine throwing arm to speak for the character of his heart. This young man knows what team he is on. Interviewed in the *Utah Journal* newspaper in November 1989, Ty said: "Because people know who I am, I feel as if I have to set high standards. It might sound corny, but I've signed the Honor Code here, and I'm not supposed to be doing certain things. If I did those things, my reputation would suffer." I was not surprised when Ty entered the waters of baptism on February 6, 1991, joining the same spiritual team you and I are on.

Do we remember the Honor Code that we accepted at baptism? Are we as strong in protecting the image we present to those who watch us as Ty Detmer is? Do we remember the scripture in 2 Timothy 1:7, which reads, "For God hath not given us the spirit of fear; but of power, and of love, and of a sound mind." As we choose positive attitudes and positive actions, God will give us the power to follow through.

A young missionary was picked up at the bus station by his zone leaders on his first day in the mission field. He was taken directly to a discussion; and when the gentleman opened the door, not two elders were standing there, but three. This man was a chronic investigator. He had been taught by every set of Elders for a dozen years, and he could lip sync the discussions. His sweet wife kept inviting the missionaries back, and they came, but with little progress. Little progress until this Elder stepped through his door.

The man later said he did not know whether the missionary told him his name or not. The young Elder sat in a corner of this investigator's living room staring at his shoes and cowering in terror throughout the entire discussion. Meanwhile the investigator stared at him. The man gave a portion of his attention to the zone leaders who were reciting the discussions, and if they missed a word, he would correct them, but his attention was focused on the youngest missionary hovering in the corner.

As the man observed the scene, an inner dialogue went on inside his mind: Why is this young man on a mission? If he is so terrified, why did he come? The answer was simple, and the man heard it plainly. He came because he knows the Church is true. The man stated later, "I don't know if that young man was responsible for another baptism during his entire mission, but he was responsible for mine." God does not give us the spirit of fear, but of power and of love, and a sound mind. This terrified Elder knew which team he was on, and I feel certain that the promise in 2 Timothy was fulfilled in him, and that he became a powerful missionary as a blessing for having exercised his faith.

We must someday come to act upon the promises our Father in Heaven has made to us, calling down the power that is available if we will pay the price. There are so many distractions pulling us away from our focus that it is easy to forget why we are here and whom we serve.

Long ago when the Jews were in captivity in Babylon, several Jewish youth were given the opportunity to receive leadership training, and later three of them, Shadrach, Meshach, and Abednego, were appointed to rule "over the affairs of the province of Babylon" (Daniel 2:49). Nebuchadnezzar, the king, caused a huge golden image to be made and gave instructions to all his people that when they heard the sound of music announcing the setting up of the golden image, they had to fall down and worship it in full view of everyone in the crowd. Anyone who failed to bow down would be cast into a furnace and be burned to death.

Most of the Babylonians had no problem with a little bowing (under the circumstances), but it created quite a problem for our three Jewish leaders. They were not casual citizens who might "just happen to get stuck at home" and "forget to be out there in the parade." These men were equivalent to the governors, or the senators, or the king's cabinet. And their refusal to bow down would bring out the five o'clock news cameras and flash the bulletin right back to Nebuchadnezzar. Nevertheless their understanding was clear: according to Jewish law, they were to worship no God but Jehovah, or Jesus Christ.

The moment came and went, and the three Jews stood tall in a sea of bowing bodies. The king was enraged. He summoned Shadrach, Meshach, and Abed-nego to his court. "Listen," he said in front of his entire court, "I'm going to give you one more chance. Tomorrow, right before 'Good Morning, America,' you will bow down, and we'll get it on national television. If not, you will be thrown into the fiery furnace, and we will get *that* on national television." Either way, Nebuchadnezzar made sure he was going to win.

Suddenly these three men faced the same dilemma that everyone will one day face who walks the earth and professes to have a line he will not cross. Do I bite the bullet and stand for what I believe, or do I bow down "just this once" to please the crowd? The key lies in three words: *But if not.* Those faithful young men stood forth, proud and strong, and without any hesitation answered their challenge: "If it be so, our God whom we serve is able to deliver us from the burning fiery furnace, and he will deliver us out of thine hand, O king. [I can picture a slight pause here as their eyes took on the glint of steel] *But if not,* be it known unto thee, O king, that we will not serve thy gods, nor worship the golden image which thou hast set up."

There would be no compromise. They knew which team they were on. The king did throw them in the fire. It was so hot that it burned to death the soldiers who had to throw them into it. But Shadrach, Meshach, and Abed-nego walked around in the fire with a fourth who attended them. The king and all his princes and governors witnessed this remarkable miracle. When the men finally were called out of the fire, there was not even the smell of smoke on their clothes. (See Daniel 3:1–27.)

When they made their decision they did not know what the Lord would do, but they knew what *they* had to do.

Abinadi, the brave prophet whose story is in the book of Mosiah, was caught in a similar situation. If he fulfilled his mission and denounced King Noah, he faced a fiery death at the stake. Did a "fourth" walk him out of the flames? No. Abinadi burned, prophesying to the end as the fire ate away his flesh. (See Mosiah 17:13–20.) God could have delivered him; Abinadi knew that. "But if not," Abinadi still knew which team he was on, and he *would not cross the line.*

As trials and temptations come to us, we can control our reaction to them. We cannot always control our circumstances, but we can choose how we will react. Choosing to be positive and happy and faithful is power. In 1982 I learned that lesson.

It was a Saturday morning in May when I drove my eight-year-old daughter, Tarisse, to the doctor's office. She had an ear infection. The physician wrote out the prescription, and we were on our way.

In the movies when something dramatic is going to happen, what changes? The music. There is no music in real life, so as I approached the car, I heard nothing. As I climbed in, the words came into my head, "Tell Tarisse to put on her seatbelt." I thought the words were my own thoughts, and I repeated them aloud. Tarisse obeyed. The words could have said, "Why don't you get the prescription filled at this pharmacy and save yourself another stop?" Or they could have invited me to turn right at the street corner and go to the mall and buy myself some new shoes. I would have liked that one. They didn't. Instead, the words in my mind simply invited me to ask my daughter to fasten her seatbelt. The ride was about to get very bumpy.

As I pulled up to the traffic light just outside the physician's parking lot, the light was flashing red. I treated it like a four-way stop sign. I waited my turn, and then I went. Two cars were yielding to me on the right and on the left, and the car opposite me entered the intersection. I pulled across in my turn. What I could not see because of a huge advertising sign in my line of vision was a car approaching from my left in the fast lane whose driver did not intend to yield right of way. She struck both vehicles, hitting me at 55 miles per hour and pushing my car forty feet into the pole that supported the traffic light.

Because of her seatbelt, my daughter was held firmly and safely in place and received no injuries besides a bump on her forehead. The driver's side of the door, however, crushed in twenty-two inches and literally folded me in half. My pelvis was broken in six places, two splinters breaking off it and piercing my bladder. They lacerated my spleen, shredded my diaphragm, and scraped my colon. Five ribs were broken, both lungs collapsed, and a motor nerve in the base of my skull was bruised. That paralyzed half my tongue, so that I could not feel or control that half. I could swallow with half my tongue but the other half oozed out whatever I was eating. I could talk with half my tongue, and the other half sounded like teeth stuck with putty. I received a sprained back and a sprained neck. I was not in the best shape.

One of the physicians who operated on me had passed the accident on his way home. When he had looked at my car he concluded that no one had lived through that collision. His phone was ringing when he walked in the door at home, and he headed back to the operating room, where he was one of the six men who spent four hours putting Humpty Dumpty back together again. For eight days they told my family that I might not live. The lung equipment available five years earlier would not have been sophisticated enough to keep me alive. The head surgeon told me later that if the emergency services in Albuquerque had not worked exactly as they were supposed to, I would not have made it to the hospital alive.

My memory did not return for ten days. When I did awaken, I was looking at the wall in my room. I knew right away that I was not at home, because the wall was too clean. Then I recognized that I was in a hospital. I had had four children. However, I did not now remember being pregnant, and so I wondered *why* I was in the hospital. I couldn't feel anything; I had no idea that I was injured. I started to turn my face to see if there was anyone in the room who could explain what was going on, and in doing so I was suddenly filled with a hot, firelike swirling in my arms and legs. Tears sprang to my eyes as words came to my mind. I could hear them plainly, if silently. "Kathy," they began, "you need not fear. You will be perfectly all right." Even with that incredible comfort, I still had to go through the process of healing. The Lord does not give us the spirit of fear, but of power, and I was about to learn all about that.

On my first morning home from the hospital my two-year-old son came and woke me up. He was hungry. My poor husband had served double duty for two weeks, and so I let him sleep and made my way into the kitchen to feed my son. I need to let you envision the picture. The muscles that wrapped around the broken pelvis were totally non-functional, and though I could shuffle my feet along while using a walker, I could not lift my feet or legs at all. Also, hooked onto the side of my walker was a portable friend. An injured bladder creates the need for such a friend, and everywhere I went people could tell whether I had been drinking enough fluids.

I shuffled my way into the kitchen, and it was not until I was there that it occurred to me that I could not take my hands off my walker to reach up and get down a bowl, to open the refrigerator to take out the milk or the eggs. My son was impatient and ready to eat, and I suddenly felt completely useless.

I was headed back down the hall to waken my exhausted husband when I just melted into a pile of tears. I thought to myself, Poor me. And you would have agreed. My head was shaven because the car had lifted off one-third of my scalp; my tongue was slobbery; I had wounds from exploded glass in my arm; I had scars everywhere from the tubes that had gone in and come out of my body to drain the internal injuries. You would have looked at me and thought: This woman has a right to feel sorry for herself. She is ugly! The Spirit did not agree. The voice came back, and the words in my mind taught me a lesson full of power. They said: "You can either be a physical wreck *and* an emotional wreck, or you can just be a physical wreck. What's it going to be?"

We are given the power to choose. We cannot choose our circumstances at all times, but we can choose how we react to those circumstances. Have you ever known someone who said: "Don't talk to me in the morning. I'm just not a morning person"? Or who said, "That's just the way I am"? Whether it is a bad temper, or being shy, or not wanting to stand up for what they know to be true, people who give in to negatives are choosing to be unhappy. Choosing to be positive is power.

Heavenly Father does not abandon us during those toughest moments of trial and inner struggle. In my case, this was one of the most spiritually tender moments of my life. A few short days after being released from the hospital it was time to get my buttons and my stitches removed. My stitches had literally been reinforced with fourteen one-inch mother-of-pearl buttons, which were sewn down both sides of my abdomen. Because my lungs had collapsed, the physicians were concerned that I would contract pneumonia and that my coughing would rip out the stitches holding my incision closed. So they sewed a button on one side of the incision, sewed down through the incision going across my tummy, and then came up through another button on the other side. My scars are very personalized. My tummy looks like a zipper and buttonholes.

The day they were to be removed my girlfriend drove me to the surgeon's office and dropped me off while she parked. I could not lift my legs, as I've said, so I set my walker down and dragged my feet: walker down, shuffle, shuffle; walker down, shuffle, shuffle. It was the longest hallway I had ever seen in my life. I made my way down it, turned into the doctor's office, and then waited for my turn.

When one's pelvis is broken in six places there are not many comfortable positions. So I would stand for a few minutes and then I would sit for a few minutes, and I rotated that combination over and over while I waited. Finally the pain became pretty intense. Then I saw my surgeon pass the doorway. "Dr. Feder," I began, with the painted-on smile that I wore now that I had chosen to be only a physical wreck. "I either need a pain pill or a doctor!" My cheery tone was a high falsetto.

He looked at me and gasped in horror. "How long have you *been* there?"

"An hour," I chirped, with my bright smile.

He ushered me immediately into one of the rooms, removed my decorations, checked to make sure all systems were "go," and then sent me down the long hallway again to meet my friend with her car.

About two-thirds of the way down the hall my legs quit working. The muscles froze, and I simply could not get them to shuffle or pull anymore. I was stuck. I considered my alternatives: I could get down on my hands and knees and crawl back to the doctor's office, dragging my portable friend alongside me, and ask for a wheelchair to wheel the gimp out to her car. Or I could stand there and scream until someone heard me and brought a wheelchair.

With ten days' amnesia followed by only a few days' memory of the whole episode, I was not emotionally ready for either of those alternatives. I held onto the sides of my walker while I bowed my head and begged: "Oh, Father, please! Please make my legs work. I don't care about the pain—I can handle that, but please don't make me crawl back to that office." I closed my prayer in the name of Jesus Christ, and immediately the pain vanished and my legs unfroze. I could move. Now, I did not throw my walker in the air and lift my arms, crying, "Hallelujah, brother, I'm healed!" but it was as much a miracle to me as if that is what happened. *I knew where that power had come from.*

In what may seem to be the darkest of times, if we will but reach up to our Father (instead of away from him to alternative counterfeits) he will hold our hand through the ordeal. It may be that he will tenderly lead us out of the "flames." *But if not,* we must still demonstrate which team we are on in each decision each day of our lives. And there is a "Heisman trophy" waiting for each one of us who endures to the end while remaining focused on the goal.

Kathryn S. Smith, a middle-school teacher (English and French) in Provo, Utah, has four children. Among her interests are writing, theater, and horseback riding. In 1966 she toured around the world in ninety days. In getting through her teen years Kathy was helped by knowing she was "someone who mattered; I didn't give in to the magnets pulling me in different directions."

5

The Dating Game: For Whom the Phone Tolls

Randall C. Bird

At each session of EFY several classes on dating are offered in your program. I've often wondered why so many youth attend each of these classes. Is it in the hopes that they will improve their dating rating? Is it so they can just meet each other and start a new romance here at EFY? (I guess the new term is not just "meet each other" but "scope out" the youth in attendance in hopes of finding the perfect "ten.") Whatever the reason, let me state to begin with that after you have read this chapter your phone probably will not start ringing off the hook because of the people calling you for dates, nor will reading this solve all the problems you may be having in dating. But it will give some new ideas and ways to have fun on dates so that you can properly prepare for the most important event in your life—that of marriage in the house of the Lord.

Now, in this chapter I'm going to cover three basic things about dating: First, when to date. Second, how to get a date. (That's kind of important, isn't it?) Third, what to do on a date.

As to when, President Spencer W. Kimball stated: "Life is not wholly for fun and frolic. It is a most serious business. . . . Any dating or pairing off in social contacts should be postponed until at least the age of sixteen or older." (*Ensign*, February 1975, p. 4.)

Now, isn't that counsel easy to follow? Sure it's simple—until some beautiful girl or some handsome guy asks you out prior to your sixteenth birthday. At that point you might begin to say: "Let's see. I'm fifteen and a half, very mature for my age, Mom and

Dad will probably let me go if I want to." Now this counsel from a prophet has become crucial in your life. You have to make what you consider to be a major decision. Of course, after you become a senior in high school or get to college age you can look back and even laugh at the turmoil and trouble you went through in making the decision whether to date prior to sixteen. Many young people have stated that, as they look back now, whether to date prior to sixteen really wasn't a "biggie." So the hard part is when you're right there making that decision.

As a parent, here's how I would teach my children about waiting to date until they are sixteen. I would reach over and get the portable blackboard that every mother makes in Relief Society, write the number 8 on it, and say, "What important event happens when you're eight years old?" And my children would say, "Baptism." Good, that's right! Now, if any of my children are only 7¾ years old, can they be baptized? No. And who said that we should wait until eight years of age to be baptized? The Lord gave us that counsel through the Prophet Joseph Smith, and it is recorded in the Doctrine and Covenants (see D&C 68:27).

Next I would draw a parallel to baptism at age eight by writing the number 16 on the blackboard and asking, "What important event happens when we turn sixteen?" Many will respond, "We get our driver's license." The answer we are looking for is, "We get to date." That's right, we have the opportunity of dating at the age of sixteen. And who said we should wait until sixteen to date? It is the prophets who have counseled us to wait until sixteen. So when we say waiting until sixteen to date is dumb and stupid, who are we really saying is dumb and stupid? At this point my teenagers are ready to attack me and make the traditional teenage statement, "But that isn't fair!"

Now, here's Brother Bird's guess as to some reasons why we should wait until the age of sixteen to date.

Every one of us has what I call the "need for new experiences" in his life. This need seems to start right after birth. So, as a little child, you get on your tricycle and ride down the driveway, causing much excitement inside you. It feels neat, this new experience of riding a tricycle.

But after a while, merely riding the tricycle just doesn't give you the same feeling it used to, so you say to yourself, "I have the need for a new experience." Then at the age of three you yell out to your brothers, sisters, and parents, "Mom, Dad, come look!" With your family staring at you, you soar down the driveway with your hands removed from the tricycle, bringing great excitement to yourself and your audience. You're excited because your body has just had a new experience, one it hadn't felt before.

This need for new experiences continues as you grow older and receive a bicycle. Soon it's just not cool to ride a bike all the time using both hands. You feel a need to be able to ride without holding the handlebars, leaning left or right to turn. It's a new experience to fold your arms and turn corners—especially if you hit a rock.

What about a motorbike? Do we need new experiences as we ride them? Sure! Everyone can ride one with both wheels on the road, but when we can stand them up, up on one wheel—what a thrill! And it has met our need for a new experience. This continues even into cars, where some have to do some daring thing to achieve what they feel is a new experience. It could range from taking the shocks off and bouncing around in the road to seeing how fast the car can travel. All these things fulfill the need for new experiences.

You ought to take note that in virtually all the above "new experiences"—which in each case are so exciting at the time—there is an element of potential danger. From the kid on the tricycle up to the final event in our transportation story there is the risk of the driver's losing control of the machine, with possible injurious results of one degree or another. In fact, such accidents are happening every day, and in every case they are a surprise to the driver—he hadn't perceived the hidden dangers.

Now let's look at the need for new experiences in dating. Here you must pretend with me that you are going on a first date. Boys are great as they get ready for dates. Sometimes a boy will pretend to shave and will splash on a little "Eternity for Men" cologne, as this is a big event in his life. Let's follow a young man and woman as they go on their date and meet the needs for new experiences in their lives.

The young man pulls up to the girl's house, gets out of the car, and walks toward the front door. He nervously rings the doorbell, and suddenly there appears the most beautiful girl he's ever seen —his date. The girl invites him in to meet all the family—and I mean all the family. He meets Mom and Dad, brothers and sisters, aunts and uncles, and even the family pet.

Following this, the couple proceeds to the car. The young man, being a gentleman, opens the door and lets the girl in on her side of the car, then goes around the car to his side and puts himself behind the steering wheel.

Now comes a new experience. As he looks toward his date, he notices that she is scooting toward him. She scoots all the way over and sits next to him, which she thinks of as the polite thing to do. But girls, can you imagine how that makes a young man feel? He is in seventh heaven! His heart beats faster, and he wonders why his mother never told him about this moment. This is a new experience, and it should be remembered that these feelings are good.

They are God-given, and when used properly they lead to nothing but happiness.

Now one of the major decisions of the young man's life lies before him: This beautiful girl is seated next to me. Do I hold her hand?

Boys, there are international signs that let you know when a girl is ready to hold your hand. Look at the girl seated next to you and notice her hands. If they are folded "snugly and tight," she has no interest in holding hands. If, however, her hand is just resting upon her leg or lap, it is available to hold. At a youth conference in Arkansas I asked girls whether there are clues a girl gives to let the boy know she would like to hold his hand. After we had received a lot of interesting clues, one young lady spoke up and said, "You can put your hand on the clutch." Obviously she was not well acquainted with cars, and her response brought the audience to total laughter. The girl's hand on the clutch certainly would be a clue (to say nothing of its producing a new experience), though there are better ones to use.

But let's get back to the young man in the car. Suppose he decides to hold the girl's hand. He reaches down, takes the girl by the hand — and then the fireworks begin. Inside his body now are emotions and feelings he has never before experienced. Simultaneously, the same kind of thing is happening to the girl seated next to him. These feelings are sometimes easily mistaken to be love, but it should be noted that this couple is just having a new experience — and it feels very pleasant.

Now, let's assume that these two continue to date several more times. After a while the young man finds out that holding hands no longer brings out the emotions it did earlier; so in his mind he says, "I have the need for a new experience." This time he desires to put his arm around the girl; so, while driving the car with one hand, he tries the age-old yawn-and-stretch routine. This causes his right arm to stretch around the back of the girl, coming to rest on her shoulder.

Girls, if this happens to you, you now have a major decision to make: Do I let this hand stay on my shoulder, or do I pick it up, bring it back around to the boy, and ask, "Excuse me, is this yours?" If you allow the boy's arm to stay around you, this in turn causes those same feelings to return that were previously experienced while holding hands. As they do, his heart beats faster, your heart beats faster, and again it's all very pleasant.

As the dating continues, you'll find that before long the holding of hands, the arm around the girl — these no longer evoke those special feelings you felt earlier. Therefore, in his mind the young man once again says, "I have the need for a new experience." And here we get to the goodnight kiss.

An author I have not been able to identify wrote:

Kissing

Before I heard the doctors tell
the dangers of a kiss,
I had considered kissing you
the nearest thing to bliss.
But now I know Biology
and sit and sigh and moan—
Six million bacteria,
and I thought we were alone.

To be serious again, I must emphasize that kissing is meant to be a very sacred and special experience. Having coached football for many years, I have observed many young men, and it saddens my heart to hear some of them talk about the way they go out and kiss girls as though it were a contest. You young brothers and sisters would do well to follow the counsel of President Spencer W. Kimball in which he said: "Kissing [should] be saved at least until these later hallowed courtship days when they could be free from sex and have holy meaning." (*The Miracle of Forgiveness* [Salt Lake City: Book-craft, 1969], p. 231.) And again: "A kiss is an evidence of affection. It is an evidence of love, not an evidence of lust. . . . I don't mind your kissing each other after you have had several dates, but not the Hollywood kiss, not the kiss of passion, but the kiss of affection, and there won't be any trouble. Now, remember these things." (From an address given at Brigham Young University to returned missionaries, January 2, 1959.)

The reason why "there won't be any trouble" is that you won't have lost control. It's like the escalating of the new experiences in our transportation story—at any point the young driver might lose control, but when his pulse is racing with the "thrill" of the wild-speeding car the danger is usually greatest. In your dating, then, be content with the milder, "lawful" pleasures, and avoid the escalation. In this way you can always be in control of your feelings, and you'll be out of danger. You can then look forward to enjoying with the Lord's approval and blessing the special, sacred experience of married love that awaits you down the road.

You see, the need for new experiences continues, but if you handle your experiences wisely they will lead to a proper marriage. Then you will have the opportunity of becoming one with your marriage partner in helping to bring to earth choice spirits from the presence of our Heavenly Father. What a beautiful thing when done properly, as his prophets counsel us! What a new experience to enjoy, with nothing to regret, no guilt feelings! I feel that this is why we've been counseled to wait until sixteen before dating — so that we can properly develop emotionally, physically, and spiritually, and thus be able to handle life's new experiences in a righteous manner rather than after the ways of the world.

Well, having waited for the right age to get a date, it would be nice if you had one. I would now like to give you Brother Bird's four steps to getting a date. These four steps are guaranteed to work — some of the time. Since boys can just go on inviting girls out until they get an acceptance, these steps are designed for girls to use, even though they can be used by boys as well.

Step number 1. The old stare-at-'em routine. Here's the way it works. A handsome young man walks into your math class and is headed towards his seat. As he approaches you, you stare at him. Now, by stare at him I don't mean you look as if in some hypnotic trance, gazing off into never-never land. I mean the type of look that picques the young man's curiosity. Note that to be valid, this look must be taught by mothers, Young Women advisors, and other certified instructors. It's the type of look in which you kind of glance in his direction and then look away. It's a now-you-see-it, now-you-don't type of look. After you've done that, the young man will go to his seat and in his mind say (as he stares at the floor), "I wonder if that girl is still looking at me." After a short pause he will raise his head, only to find that you are still looking in his direction. This has caused eyes to meet eyes for a split second, and curiosity has been aroused.

It would be wise for the young man at this point *not* to rise from his seat, go to the girl and say, "I noticed that you were staring at me. Would you like to go out Friday night?" Most girls would respond, "Oh, I wasn't staring at you." So, they continue to play the old "hard to get" routine. Needless to say, this brief stare or look has attracted some attention.

Step number 2. Be where he is. This step gives you a chance to attend a church event, a high school extra-curricular event, or even a community event and be where he is. In college it was fun, because you could go to the computer and find out a person's class schedule. With that class schedule, you could just happen to be by the right building when that person would be exiting. As he walked by, he would see you, and again in his mind he'd say, "Whoa, wasn't that the girl who was staring at me in math class the other day?" Again, you have caused the young man to think about you. He noticed you in class and has noticed you again in a different environment. You are now ready to move on to step 3, the most-used step in the dating world.

Step number 3. Tell a friend. It works something like this. Two girls come together and this is their conversation: "Julie, do you know who I'm dying to go out with?" Julie answers by saying, "No, who?" Whereupon the first girl says, "Do you promise not to tell?" Now, the last thing the first girl wants is for Julie to keep it secret. She's hoping that Julie will run immediately to someone and spread this information. Anyway, Julie responds with, "I promise." The first girl then reveals that she is dying to go out with Shawn. Now, after hearing that information Julie will run to either Shawn or Shawn's best friend and spread the exciting news that her best friend is dying to go out with Shawn. Isn't that the way it works? Of course it is.

Now, if after step 3 you do not have a date, you probably should give up on this one person. He will have noticed you, the word will have been spread, and he apparently is not interested. The other possibility is that he is too shy. If you feel this is the case, you could move on to step 4.

Step number 4. Ask him out. It would be perfectly legal for a girls'-choice event to ask him out. There's nothing more fun than having a group of girls plan a date from beginning to end and then execute that plan. Sometimes the plan even works. Girls are so creative in how they ask someone out, and the evening's activities are usually hilarious. This would allow you to have a great time in a group situation, which is surely the best way to date in high school.

Well, now that you're old enough to date, and you have a date, it would be good to discuss briefly what you ought to be doing on dates. You just heard me mention that I would date in groups as much as possible in high school. You're able to do things in groups that just can't be done if you pair off. For example, suppose you want to have a Chinese fire drill with the group that's in your car. You stop the car, open the doors, yell "fire drill!" and everyone runs around the car chasing one another. Now, if there were just two of you in the car and the police saw you chasing the girl around the car, they might throw you in jail. You see, they would think you were strange, whereas with the other group they would say, "Oh, it's only those Mormons out on another strange date."

I remember on one occasion taking my priests quorum to a neighboring community, where they were to learn about some professions they could at some time consider as possible careers. As we entered this city of about forty thousand people, my quorum challenged me to lead out in a Chinese fire drill. I explained how stupid it would be for me, their leader and bishop, to lead out in such an activity, but they continued to pester me to lead out. After several pleadings I gave in to the group pressure and opened my door and started to run around my car. Much to my chagrin, the others in the car closed the door and pulled away, leaving me in the road. How embarrassing! Me, a bishop in The Church of Jesus Christ of Latter-day Saints, standing in the middle of the road a victim of a teenage prank. After I had waited several minutes for the priests to return, they came around the corner, rolled down the window, and asked, "Are you looking for a ride?" I responded, "Yes!!" Whereupon they answered, "Hope you find one," and drove away. Then they came back around the corner again and picked me up, and we continued to have an enjoyable evening together.

Groups are an excellent way to get to know other people and to keep conversations going, and usually they allow you to come home with fond memories and not guilt feelings. I would also encourage you as youth to date those people who hold to the standards of the gospel, which are so important in developing relationships that could last for eternity.

May the Lord continue to bless you in your many decisions and choices. I know that even though we've had some fun with the topic of dating it is a serious subject that can involve eternal consequences for choices made. I pray that you'll have a constructive attitude toward your homes, your schools, your Church, and toward other people generally. If you'll do those things you'll grow up free from the contamination the world gives and you'll have eternal life —the type of life that God himself lives.

Randall C. Bird, a seminary principal and teacher in Shelley, Idaho, has served as a track and football coach and has been listed in Who's Who in America. *He likes fishing, sports, collecting sports cards and memorabilia, and reading. In high school he was named to the Idaho all-state teams in football and track. Randall and his wife, Carla, have six children.*

6

The Second Coming and You

Curtis L. Jacobs

Every time I have the chance to address young people like yourselves I try to imagine the various experiences you've had in
your lives. I see your smiles, your struggles, and your desire to do
the right. I think of my own children. I remember some of the great
events in their lives. And I can't help but remember some of the
crazy things they've done.

One evening we were just about to have dinner. It was the first
time my wife had prepared this particular dish, and we were all
looking at her new delicacy, not quite sure what we should do with
it. Anyway, it was our five-year-old son Joshua's turn to give the
prayer. I said, "Go ahead and say the prayer, Joshua." He paused,
bowed his head, and prayed, "Dear Heavenly Father, *please* help us
eat this stuff, even though we don't like it, so Mom won't be mad."
I feel pretty confident that's not what my wife expected.

Another incident: Our daughter Sarah was just learning how to
sew. Joshua sat watching her, amazed. He walked over and asked if
she could sew his finger. Sarah thought about it and said, "Sure."
So Joshua put his index finger right under the needle and said,
"O.K., let's see." Sarah pushed on the foot pedal and, sure enough,
she was able to sew right through his finger—about five times.
Ouch! She has always tried to be so helpful for her brothers.

Finally, there is our Jonathan. While my wife was over at a
friend's house, helping with the sewing, there came a scream from
their family room. One of the daughters of my wife's friend in-

formed everybody, "He's killed it." The "it" was the family's pet hamster. Evidently Jonathan had gone into the room where the hamster cage was, opened it, and tried to hold the little critter. Well, if you've ever tried to do that, you know that hamsters aren't very keen on the idea. The hamster must have started scratching at Jonathan, who figured that if he just held it tight enough it would quit scratching. Well, he held it tighter and tighter until . . . well, it finally stopped scratching. It stopped doing anything. When it stopped moving, Jonathan (being a very quick child) realized something was wrong. He put it back into the cage and left the room. When everything had finally come to light, my wife came up to him, hoping to see remorse. With everyone looking at this little three-year-old, my wife said, "Jonathan, what did you do?" With a gleam in his eye and excitement in his voice, he said, "I killed it!" Now, that's remorse.

I have to wonder how my children are going to be as teenagers. Why do they do some of the dumb things they do? Why do any of us?

To help answer that question, let's briefly review an old black-and-white movie, *Random Harvest*, which Truman Madsen discussed in a similar context in his book *The Highest in Us* (Bookcraft, 1978). It's one of those movies that throws a few extra curves at you.

The story begins in an asylum, in England, where a young Englishman has been brought. It's during World War I. While serving in Europe he has been "shell shocked"—he can't remember anything; it's a complete memory loss. While there in the asylum, he yearns to belong to somebody. An older couple comes by, checking whether he is their son. They enter the room where he sits alone, look at him, then turn away disappointed.

One evening, suddenly everyone is celebrating—the war has ended. No one stops him as he walks out of the gate. He finds himself in town and enters a little shop. There he meets Paula, who realizes he is from the asylum and is determined to help him. In time they marry and have a son.

"Smithy" wants to become a writer. With a manuscript prepared, he goes to Liverpool to deliver it. It's the first time he has left Paula. (You can tell something is going to happen.) In Liverpool he is hit by a cab. Here comes the movie's first curve: suddenly his memory of life before he became shell-shocked returns; but now he can't remember anything that has happened to him since that point. He is no longer "Smithy," or John Smith, but Charles Rainier. To him there is no Paula, no marriage, no son.

He returns to his family and his former status. He runs for Parliament and gets elected. Paula sees his picture in a paper. When he sees her, he doesn't remember her. She determines she wants to stay near him, so she becomes his secretary. After a while another curve is thrown — he asks her to marry him. It's not to be a real marriage, but just for social requirements, because the two work so well together. He calls the marriage a "merger." She is advised not to marry him, but does. It doesn't turn out as she had hoped. One night he presents her with a very expensive gift, a beautiful emerald. She takes it, runs into her room, and takes out a piece of cheap jewelry he had given her as "Smithy" when their son was born. She determines to take a long vacation, maybe to leave him for good.

He takes her to the railway station before leaving on a business trip with an associate to the same town where the asylum is. As far as he knows, he's never been there before. While in that town, he says to his friend, "Let's go into this little shop." His friend asks, "How do you know about a little shop?" His memory seems to be returning. They determine to try to help him retrace his life there.

He finds himself a little way out of town at the old cottage where he used to live with Paula. He reaches in his pocket and takes out an old key he has had with him all this time. He enters the front gate of the cottage, goes up to the door, takes out the key. It fits.

Having heard that he was in town, Paula has followed him to the cottage and arrives at this point. She rushes up to the gate. While his back is to her, she calls out, "Smithy." Struck by that name, he turns. Again she says, "Smithy." You can tell his entire memory is returning and he knows her now for what she really is to him. "Paula," he calls out, and they rush into each other's arms. (The girls always love that part. The guys go out for popcorn.)

Why do I tell this story? Because we all have been "shell-shocked." We can't remember our former existence in the presence of "noble and great ones." There we lived with the King of Heaven — God, our Heavenly Father. But because we can't now remember our life there we stumble and fall here. We make mistakes, some small, some maybe not so small. We desperately try to belong to someone, perhaps to anyone. Each of us tries to fit into the world and find his "true" self.

The problem comes in the way some young people try to fit into the world. Some try to be "cool," "macho," whatever you want to call it. I remember going to my first year of college. I wanted to be a part of it all. I went to a joint fraternity/sorority party. There I found the "cool" guys (some of them were returned missionaries) and the "cool" ladies drinking—a few were even using drugs. I'd never seen this before. I saw some of the guys go into the bathroom, sick from drinking so much. This was supposed to be cool?

A special edition of *Newsweek* magazine (Summer/Fall 1990) was dedicated to "The New Teens . . . What Makes Them Different." It talked about many of the problems and decisions facing today's teenagers. One section dealt with their "heroes," or role models. Some that were mentioned there weren't bad, but the inclusion of certain others gives cause for concern. Another section dealing with "The New Rules of Courtship," contained a graph that showed metropolitan areas of the USA for 1988. This map indicated that by age nineteen some 78 percent of girls have lost their virtue, while for young men it was 86 percent. Today youth are surrounded by sexual temptations. One of the saddest times I've faced as a teacher is when a beautiful young LDS girl or good-looking guy comes to me having tried to find happiness in being immoral. They find themselves paying a much higher price than they ever imagined. The world has lied to them in movies, music, and the printed page. "Wickedness never was happiness."

A few months ago Arsenio Hall was interviewing Warren Beatty (of "Dick Tracy" fame). Hall asked Beatty about his co-star, Madonna. Beatty said, "Everybody loves Madonna." I started thinking about the number of young people who, in trying to find themselves, are lost in trying to be a "Madonna."

A high school in Utah which is heavily Mormon, allows its graduating seniors to list their goals for the next ten years, or for life. What would you show for your goals? One young man wrote: "I will be working very hard at whatever I am doing, but there is one thing I know for sure: I am going to be very well known throughout the nation and possibly the world." (Humble, huh?) Another wrote: "To bring the world into a whirlwind of decadence, chaotic anarchy, and social downfall that will result in the destruction of mankind." (Now, that's the kind of kid I'd want to bring home to Mom and Dad.) One girl wrote, "Divorced and fat, sitting on a couch eating chocolates while watching 'Days of our Lives.' " One ambitious girl wrote, "Announcing the blue-light specials at K Mart." Many mentioned that their goal in life was to be rich—not just a millionaire, one said, but a billionaire. Compare these to one who said: "I would like to be working with handicapped children; working with them in physical education. I would also like to learn and teach sign language. I would also like to be married and have children."

What does all the above have to do with you and the Second Coming? Here is part of a talk given by President Ezra Taft Benson to over 8,500 seminary and institute students in California: "While our generation will be comparable in wickedness to the days of Noah, when the Lord cleansed the earth by flood, there is a major difference this time: God has saved for the final inning some of His stronger and most valiant children, who will help bear off the kingdom triumphantly. . . . You are the generation that must be prepared to meet your God." (*Ensign*, April 1987, p. 73.) How much of what the world would have you do is preparing you to meet the Savior?

Now do you understand why you were born in this day? The Lord saved you to help prepare the world for the second coming of the Savior. But because we don't remember who we are and what we should be doing, we sometimes allow the world to determine that for us.

Do you understand that the most important decision you have to make is not whether or not to be rich, or famous, or "cool," or popular? Elder Boyd K. Packer said: *"I repeat, the crucial decision. . . . of life. . . . is between good and evil.* Both fame and fortune are no more essential as ingredients to true happiness in mortality than the absence of them can prevent you from achieving it. . . . Happiness will depend on what each of us does with what each has, what we learn from what we do, and what we do thereafter. These are the things that will be reviewed in the days of judgment." (*New Era*, August 1989, p. 6, italics added.)

I've often asked youth of the Church, "Assuming you live to a normal length of life, do you believe you will be alive when the Savior comes?" Most say yes. Now, lest I be misunderstood, I add that I don't know when the Second Coming is going to take place. However, some keep trying to tell us just that. A few years ago a man who had been excommunicated from the Church "prophesied" that in forty days Salt Lake City would be destroyed. They interviewed him on TV. On the fortieth day he sat watching his television to hear the news. Meanwhile, that same night, BYU held a "last-chance dance" in honor of this man. Well, the destruction didn't happen. Nevertheless many of the prophets have warned us to be prepared, for the time is short.

The scriptures tell us of the events yet to come. There will come a day when armies numbering 200,000,000 will be involved in the battle of Armageddon. Millions will be killed. The battle will rage into the streets of Jerusalem. The Lord will have two "witnesses" that will protect the Jews. They will prophesy for three and a half years. Finally, they will be killed. Their bodies will lie in the streets for three and a half days; then suddenly they will be brought back to life and ascend into heaven.

The final battle will end with the Savior appearing on the Mount of Olives (to the east of Jerusalem) and destroying many of those fighting. The Jewish people will look at their Messiah and ask: "What are these wounds in thine hands and in thy feet? Then shall they know that I am the Lord; for I will say unto them: These wounds are the wounds with which I was wounded in the house of my friends. I am he who was lifted up. I am Jesus that was crucified. I am the Son of God. And then shall they weep because of their iniquities; then shall they lament because they persecuted their king." (D&C 45:51–53. See also Revelation 11 and Zechariah 14.)

Do we understand how dreadful for the wicked the Second Coming is going to be? A few years ago my wife's sister was visiting one of her other sisters in Cheyenne, Wyoming. They were about ready to come out of a department store, heading for their car, when it started to hail. The hailstorm was so fierce that the tops of cars were damaged, and some windshields were broken. Compare that to this: "And there shall be a great hailstorm sent forth to destroy the crops of the earth" (D&C 29:16). Think of the destruction mentioned in Revelation 16:21 —"And there fell upon men a great hail out of heaven, every stone about the weight of a talent." Guess what a talent weighs. Approximately *75 pounds*. Can you imagine trying to dodge those hailstones? All it takes is one, and you're history.

Remember the movie *Raiders of the Lost Ark*? Right at the end, when they open up the ark, do you remember what happens to the guy's face? To the wicked the Lord says: "I will take vengeance upon the wicked, for they will not repent. . . . Wherefore, I the Lord God will send forth flies upon the face of the earth, which shall take hold of the inhabitants thereof, and shall eat their flesh . . . their flesh shall fall from off their bones, and their eyes from their sockets." (D&C 29:17–19.)

When I was involved in a speaking assignment in Las Vegas a few years ago, I had the opportunity to ride to and from the stake center with Daniel Ludlow of BYU. As we were coming back to our motel, we could see the Las Vegas strip all lit up, in all its glory. He looked at it and said, "This reminds me of a statement by President Brigham Young," and then he quoted the statement: "When the testimony of the elders ceases to be given, and the Lord says to them, 'Come home; I will now preach my own sermons to the nations of the earth,' . . . you will hear of magnificent cities, now idolized by the people, sinking in the earth, entombing the inhabitants." (*Journal of Discourses* 8:123.) Will it really matter then if someone has just hit the jackpot?

There are few times when all four standard works of the Church have the same scripture quoted. One example deals with the Second Coming. (See Joseph Smith—History 1:37; Malachi 4:1; 3 Nephi 25:1; D&C 29:9.) Here is what they all say: "For behold, the day cometh that . . . all the proud, yea, and all that do wickedly shall burn as stubble . . . saith the Lord of Hosts, that it shall leave them neither root nor branch." Do you realize what the "proud" and the "wicked" are losing? What are our roots and branches? Years ago a book was published called *Roots*, written by Alex Haley. It told the story of a family that started in Africa and came to America as slaves. Do you see? Those who are destroyed have no "roots," or ancestors. And "branches"? This means they will not have any posterity either. They lose their family. Finally, the Lord says to the wicked, they will be "utterly destroyed by the brightness of my coming" (D&C 5:19). The wicked may think they can get away with their wickedness, but when the Lord finally comes they won't be able to handle the heat.

However, to the righteous the Second Coming is going to be glorious. There will yet be a great group of missionaries, 144,000 that are called to "bring as many as will come to the church of the Firstborn" (D&C 77:11). We have yet to have the great council at Adam-ondi-Ahman. "At that time there will be a transfer of authority from the . . . impostor, Lucifer, to the rightful King, Jesus Christ. . . . All who have held keys will make their reports. . . . Adam will direct this judgment and then he will make his report, as the one holding the keys for this earth, to . . . Jesus Christ." (Joseph Fielding Smith, quoted in Doctrine and Covenants Institute Manual, p. 288.) Can you imagine? All prophets of all dispensations will be there. Can you picture the potential talks that could be delivered and by whom? What a great blessing!

A couple of years ago, while my family were celebrating our daughter's seventh birthday, both of my parents were driving near the center of Utah. They were involved in a head-on collision with a semitruck, and both were killed instantly. I can still remember driving the many long hours from Arizona to Utah, having to pass by where the wreck had taken place the day before. Yes, I wept many tears. My parents had returned only seven months earlier from serving a mission together. But the gospel tells me that, if they were righteous and I am found worthy, I will have the opportunity of seeing and being with them again. Those who are of a celestial nature who are alive will be caught up to meet the Savior in the air as he descends to earth. Those who have died and are celestial will be resurrected and also caught up to meet him. (See D&C 88:96–99.) Can you visualize that? Many of you have lost a loved one, a family member, or a friend, who was righteous. Think of the anticipation, the excitement of seeing them again! Do you see the difference? The wicked are left without family, the righteous are reunited in glory.

Those who are righteous will have the privilege of reigning with the Savior for the thousand years of the Millennium. The earth will return to a Garden of Eden-like state. "And the earth shall be given unto them [the righteous] for an inheritance; . . . and their children shall grow up without sin unto salvation." Can you picture having children that are always good? "And the Lord shall be in their midst." (D&C 45:58–59.)

Do you see the difference between the righteous and the wicked? Does the world really offer us what we are worth?

So how can you have a better chance of being prepared? You should all know the answer. Elder David B. Haight has said: "Though the world is becoming more wicked, the youth of Christ's church can become more righteous *if they understand who they are*, understand the blessings available, and understand the promises God has made to those who are righteous, who believe, who endure" (*Ensign*, January 1974, p. 40). And the way you understand who you are—remember we've all been "shell-shocked"—is really quite simple. Make sure you have daily personal prayer. Search the scriptures, apply their message in your life, remember it was the rod of iron that led to the tree of life. Listen to the living prophet. Seek the Holy Spirit, hearken to its promptings. Young men, prepare now to serve the Lord on a mission. You are needed, there are people prepared to hear the gospel wherever you are sent.

While my mother and father were serving their mission, they heard two Elders tell of teaching a Jewish young lady who was currently dating an LDS young man. In her journal my mother wrote: "He had just accepted a position over in Taiwan, where he had been a missionary. She felt that she must have the discussions to make up her mind about joining the Church and going with him. . . . They gave her one discussion and she said that she wanted them all the next day. So they were giving her the discussions, and afterwards she told them that as they were talking there was an 'aura' around them and she could see people looking at her from behind the missionaries; and she now asked who they were. The missionaries didn't have an answer, but went back to their apartment and prayed. . . . It was revealed to them . . . that they were her [future] children that would be born to her and this young man. They were waiting to see if she would accept the gospel. She did, and was baptized." What a blessing these young men were, and to more than just the young lady!

Yes, you are needed. In the talk by President Ezra Taft Benson mentioned earlier, he went on to say: "The final outcome is certain—the forces of righteousness will finally win. But what remains to be seen is *where* each of us personally, now and in the future, will stand in this battle—and how tall will we stand?"

Please, you of the nobility of heaven, stand up for the right. Don't allow the world to determine who you are, or what you will become. You are needed in God's service. May you rise to that need. When the Savior returns to the earth at his second coming, be sure he recognizes you as standing firmly on his side.

Curtis L. Jacobs, an institute teacher in Logan, Utah, holds a master's degree in Counseling and Guidance. He has been a seminary principal, an institute director, and a racquetball champion (Prescott, Arizona). His interests include basketball, piano, old movies, watching NCAA basketball, and Les Misérables *(the book, the music, the musical!). Curtis and his wife, Jolene, have three children.*

7

"The Spirit Speaketh the Truth and Lieth Not"

John G. Bytheway

On my desk at home sits a small chunk of concrete. It's not beautiful to look at. Its edges are not smooth and polished. You wouldn't call it colorful; it's mostly gray and black except on the flat side, where it's been sprayed with purple and red paint. It's not expensive, as some precious stones are, but it's very precious to me. This small chunk of rock and cement is a piece of the Berlin Wall.

Sometimes when I look at this little piece of history I think about all those who are now able to enjoy the blessings of freedom because the wall came down. Many East German people over the years tried to get beyond the wall. Some were successful, others were killed. Now the blessings of freedom are available to all because the wall came down.

Sometimes, without realizing what we're doing, we build walls around ourselves. We want the blessings of the gospel, but if we're not careful we shut out the Spirit of the Lord by putting up walls. Our Heavenly Father earnestly wants to get through to us, but he will not force his way in. We must bring down the walls and let him in. Elder H. Burke Peterson wrote: "As we go through life, we ofttimes build a rock wall between ourselves and heaven. This wall is built by our unrepented sins. . . . In spite of the wall we build in front of us, when we cry out to the Lord, he still sends his messages from heaven; but instead of being able to penetrate our hearts, they hit the wall that we have built up and bounce off. His messages don't penetrate, so we say, 'He doesn't hear,' or 'He doesn't answer.' Sometimes this wall is very formidable, and the great challenge of life is to destroy it, or, if you please, to cleanse ourselves, purifying this inner vessel so that we can be in tune with the Spirit." (*Ensign,* June 1981, p. 73.)

If we will bring down the walls we will be better able to receive answers to our prayers and guidance for solving our problems. The Spirit will teach us things that are not otherwise obtainable. The Spirit is a *teacher.*

The fifteen-year-old young lady who wrote the following letter was taught by the Spirit. She wrote this letter during a presentation at a youth conference. The Spirit was there to teach her, and she listened to what it said. Read carefully:

"I'm writing you cause I need to talk okay? Lately I've had a lot of problems with morality and the Word of Wisdom and my friends and family. I want to change so bad but I honestly don't know how. Yeah, I'll be fine right now while I'm here surrounded by the youth, but I'm afraid to go home to my friends. I'll change now, but when I go back I'm going back to my drinking friends and my foulmouth friends, etc.

"I can stand strong with the youth behind me but alone I'm afraid. I'm afraid I will give in. I'm afraid of what my friends might say, or will they laugh? My (kinda)* boyfriend I don't want to go back to. I don't want him to touch me or come near me or talk to me or anything! I want a guy to like me for me and not for any other reason. One that is my friend as well as my boyfriend."

*(The word *kinda* was written in later, scrunched between the other two words.)

Some time between the beginning and the end of the conference the boy she was dating changed in status from her "boyfriend" to her "kinda boyfriend," whom she didn't want to see or associate with ever again. Why? Did the speaker point at her from the pulpit and command her to change her boyfriend? No. The speaker wasn't even talking about dating. What really happened? She was in a meeting where the Spirit was present. The *Spirit* spoke softly to her heart and told her that she needed to change her situation. Fortunately, she put herself in a position to feel the Spirit (she attended the conference), and then she listened to what it was telling her deep inside—things about her life that no one else knew.

Not only will the Spirit speak to our hearts and tell us what is amiss in our lives but it will also give us the courage and strength to follow through. Many of the things we may learn from the Spirit may be hard for us to put into our lives.

Following is a letter from a young lady who attended Especially for Youth: "Thank you so much for the session of Especially for

Youth. It was one of the most inspiring weeks of my life. I hope it will not fade away. Thanks again for your work."

Big deal, right? Would you like to hear the rest of the story? This letter comes from the mother of the young lady: "How can we thank you for what you have done for our daughter? She called us when EFY was over, and was ecstatic over her experience. She said her testimony had been strengthened greatly, and that many of her prayers were answered. She took avid notes during the talks, and was grateful for the copies of the other presentations also. . . . This summer is a crucial time for our daughter, as a less-active boy with several good qualities, but not the right ones, is determined to keep her out of circulation until he can someday marry her. EFY, it appears, has given her the strength to break things off. Our cup runneth over with gratitude!"

I'd like to correct this wonderful mom, "The *Spirit*, it appears, has given her the strength to break things off." The Spirit will give you the power to change your life.

I'm sure that if you think back you can remember times when you've been taught by the Spirit. You've felt that you wanted to be a better person. Not better looking or more popular, just better. That's what happens when you bring down the walls and allow the Spirit of the Lord to enter. The Spirit reminds us of and pulls us toward our God-given potential.

Sometime in the future you'll have those feelings again. Perhaps while you're reading this book. Perhaps at a family home evening, or during a Church meeting or seminary class. Maybe during your own scripture study. When that happens, take some time and look deep into the feelings of your heart. Ask yourself some questions. What would the Lord have me do? You might ask: "Should I marry in the temple?" "Am I dating the type of person who would take me there?" You might ask: "Should I serve a mission?" "Am I keeping myself clean so that I may go?" Listen to the feelings deep in your heart. What has the Spirit told you? "For the Spirit speaketh the truth and lieth not. Wherefore, it speaketh of things as they really are, and of things as they really will be; wherefore, these things are manifested unto us plainly for the salvation of our souls." (Jacob 4:13.)

What wonderful words: "The Spirit speaketh the truth and lieth not." That is why it is so important that we *hear* what it says, and then *do* what we've heard. The Spirit is sent from God, who loves us perfectly and wants our success, so we must hear and do. "Ye are commanded in all things to ask of God, who giveth liberally; and *that which the Spirit testifies unto you even so I would that ye should do* in all holiness of heart, walking uprightly before me, considering the end of your salvation, doing all things with prayer and thanksgiving'' (D&C 46:7, italics added).

This chapter is not intended to tell you all the ways that we can sin or build walls against the Spirit—no chapter could do that. It is written in the hope that you will open your heart to the will of the Lord for your life, even if that heart has been closed for a long time. Sometimes things happen to us in our lives or in our families that make it hard for us to believe in anything anymore. The Lord does not want us to remain in darkness. He wants to help us understand. But we must bring down the walls and invite him in.

Many scriptures offer this metaphor: Seek, and ye shall find; ask, and ye shall receive; knock, and it shall be opened. There is one scripture, however, in which Jesus is on the other side of the door. *He* is the one who is patiently knocking, hoping that we will invite him in. ''Behold, I stand at the door, and knock: if any man hear my voice, and open the door, I will come in to him, and will sup with him, and he with me (Revelations 3:20).

Because of the gift of agency (which in the premortal life we fought valiantly to keep), each one of us has a door into his life and into his heart. We can choose whom to let in and whom to keep out. Satan wanted to destroy our agency (Moses 4:3). Satan would break down the door and force us to be obedient. The Savior, on the other hand, will not force us back to heaven. He won't even force open the door. Patiently, persistently, he stands at your door and knocks. While you are at school, fighting the daily battle for self-esteem and acceptance, where people are mercilessly teased because they're overweight or different or ''dumb,'' he is there knocking. When you feel alone and afraid and that nobody cares, he is there. Still. Knocking at your door. Please . . . let him in.

How sad it must make Father in Heaven to see some who willingly open other doors into their hearts while shutting the Savior out! How sad that people who fought so valiantly to keep their agency in the premortal life now seem almost eager to give it away by getting themselves addicted to drugs, alcohol, or pornography! If they could only remember who they are! Some of the other doors lead to an escape in the world, whereas the Savior offers an escape *from* the world. He will still knock. Softly, patiently, persistently, he will knock. Please . . . let him in.

Some of us feel that we can't do anything, that we haven't any great talents to offer. We see others with their good looks, their talents or social skills, and it makes it hard for us to like ourselves. Again, the answer to these feelings lies in opening the door to the Lord. Where does self-esteem really come from? Read carefully these words by Elder James E. Faust: ''I testify that as we mature spiritually under the guidance of the Holy Ghost, *our sense of personal worth, of belonging, and of identity increases.* I further testify that *I would rather have every person enjoy the Spirit of the Holy Ghost than any other association,* for they will be led by the Spirit to light and truth and pure intelligence, which can carry them back into the presence of God." ("The Gift of the Holy Ghost—A Sure Compass," *Ensign,* May 1989, p. 33, italics added.)

If I had a wish for every young person who might read this book it would be that they would make their own spiritual well-being their first priority; that they would pray each day to learn and grow in a better way than they have ever done before; that they would love God with all their heart, as he has loved them. I have met young people who are like this. I love them and I admire them. They are heroes to me.

Here's an excerpt of a letter from Rodney, one of my heroes: "I was coming home from a football game, and the group I was riding with, about five guys, knew I didn't drink or smoke because of my religion. Well, they promised that they wouldn't drink on the way up or back, so I told them: 'Thanks, I don't care what you do after, just as long as I get home safe' (joking with them). Well, on the way home they pulled out some beer, saying they couldn't resist any longer. I was stunned! They started to pass a can of beer around, taking sips or drinks. When it got to me I just calmly threw it out the window. They were shocked, but then they all decided that they didn't need it and threw the rest out the window. I knew I had done what was right."

I understand why such young people are called a chosen generation. For them, obedience is a quest and not an irritation. They don't say, "I can't drink," "I can't see R-rated movies," and so forth. They say, "I don't want to drink," "I don't want to see R-rated movies." In effect they say, "I don't want to do anything that might build a wall between me and the Lord." President Ezra Taft Benson told your seminary teachers: "I am sure you appreciate the fact that you have been given custody of some of the choicest spirits of all time. I emphasize that. These are not just ordinary spirits, but among them are some of the choicest spirits that have come from heaven. These are they who were reserved to come forth in this time to bear off the kingdom triumphant." ("The Gospel Teacher and His Message," in *Charge to Religious Educators* [Salt Lake City: Corporation of the President, 1982], p. 48.)

You are choice spirits. You have been sent to this world in a very difficult time. Every day, in temples throughout the world, prayers are offered for the youth of the Church. There will be difficult decisions for you to make in the years to come—decisions about missions, marriage, schooling, and career. Help is available. Please let the Lord help you. It is my prayer that you will immerse yourselves in the scriptures and pray fervently to your Father in Heaven, who loves you not only for what you are, but for what you may become.

Bring down the walls, and open the door. Learn to receive answers from the Spirit, which "speaketh the truth and lieth not."

John G. Bytheway, an administrator in Continuing Education at Brigham Young University, is currently working on a master's degree in Mass Communications. His interests include running, reading, playing the guitar, and all kinds of airplanes and cars. John's suggestions to youth are, "Life gets better, so don't give up; keep trying, keep hoping, keep trusting."

8

Is It Falling in Love or Growing in Love?

Mark A. Bybee

My twelve-year-old daughter came up to me one afternoon and asked if it was all right if she went with Kyle. I asked her where Kyle was going, and then I volunteered to take him wherever he wanted to go.

"Daaad," whined Micah, "you know what I mean!"

I said I didn't know but I was really curious to know, and asked if she would explain. From her explanation I concluded that going together meant holding hands and walking between classes together and possibly exchanging friendship rings. She said that Kyle had expressed love and caring.

Her mother and I explained to her that the only ring she could exchange was her CTR ring, and that if she chose to go with Kyle she would be going against the prophet's counsel and would eventually need to make decisions about early dating and morality, and make other decisions that it wouldn't be necessary to worry about if she were following the prophet. It was hard for us to do this, but we then told her that we would support her in whatever decision she made.

She went to her room, and Monica and I went to our room and fasted and prayed until Micah made her decision. Fortunately, within a half-hour she had made the decision to follow the prophet. I told her I was sure Kyle didn't know a lot about love.

What is love? In tennis if you're "love," it means you got skunked. According to the song, "Love is a many-splendored thing.'' In the movies it can happen on rooftops. All I know for sure is that love gives meaning and spice to life.

My father told me when I was young that people in love often put on rosy red glasses and then they don't see clearly. Dad said the glasses impaired their vision and wouldn't allow the young lovers to get to know each other's real personality. With these glasses on, the young lovers see things as they want them to be instead of how they really are. People owe it to themselves to take the rosy red glasses off before they get too serious. Many problems emerge when young lovers wait until after marriage to take off the rosy glasses and see things as they really are, and then work out the challenges.

"Do you believe in love at first sight?" I asked my area director. "No!" he answered, "I believe in sight at first love!" He explained that before marriage a person should have the best sight he has ever had; that he should look at all the angles—the personality attributes, the family background, the religious convictions, the role expectations, and any other thing that could lend truth to the relationship. He also said he didn't feel that "falling in love" was a good phrase to use, because no one "falls in love" if they expect it to last. Love should be something that grows every day through trials and happiness, through togetherness and separation, through time and eternity.

What is the world's idea of love? What would Satan have you believe concerning love? For every good force the Lord has placed on this earth, Satan has placed a counterfeit to confuse us and cause us to stumble. The counterfeit of love is lust. Lust is selfish, while love is selfless. Lust is taking something of value, while love is never taking that which is sacred and eternal. Lust is only physical, while love is emotional and spiritual. Lust is now and love is forever. Lust is of Satan and love is of God.

I once read a story about an experiment President Spencer W. Kimball asked a young couple to go through. After reading the story I decided to use the experiment as often as possible and to relate it to all my classes in hopes that other couples who thought they were "in love" would try the experiment.

In one of the cities in which I taught, I noticed two young people always hanging all over each other everywhere they went, so I told them the story and challenged them to try the experiment. The experiment consists of going for two weeks without either touching the other. They were not to hold hands, kiss goodnight, sit close together, or anything like those things. *Not touch each other! Period!* For two weeks. The purpose was to see whether they had anything in common or anything to communicate about, or whether their relationship was entirely physical. The couple was willing to do this experiment because they really thought they were "in love."

After only three days the young man came to my office and said: "She's an air-head! She can't even think for herself." The next day the girl came in and said: "He's an egotistical jerk! He thinks he's the world's gift to women." They both discovered that their relationship was only physical and that they really had nothing of eternal significance in common. I suggest this same experiment for any couple who thinks they're in love, especially if the relationship is physical.

What, then, is love—really? Love may be a lot of things, but in my limited sixteen years of marriage I have come up with a few feelings about what love is: Love is wanting to give without thinking about the receiving. Love is wanting to be together because of friendship and companionship and wanting to share. Love is the realization that your loved one is your hero and is truly "the wind beneath your wings." Love is caring, fulfilling needs, and cherishing. Love is communication at its best. Love is honesty with the loved one without fear of rejection. Love is emotional dependency. Love is wanting the best for the beloved and the fulfillment of his or her highest potential.

Last year I had an experience in one of my classes that I thought taught me, as well as all who were present, another lesson on love. Kirk knocked on my classroom door and asked if he could come in and ask a girl to one of the main dances at the school. Kirk was a state champion wrestler, a football player, and a handsome, popular athlete with whom any girl would love to have a date.

As Kirk wandered around the room—back and forth, up and down the aisle, with the roses in his hand—he recited a poem of love and caring and a desire to take a particular girl to the dance. Every girl watched with anticipation as he strolled towards her, and then with forlorn expression as he passed her by.

The most bright-eyed girl in the room was Becky, not because of anticipation on her own behalf but because of her love for life, her caring for all the other girls in the class, and her excitement for these types of curious activities in the classroom. Anticipation for herself was the furthest thing from her mind—she had been confined to a wheelchair for many years because of a long-term disease. Her eyes glistened and her smile broadened as Kirk continued to pace around the room and recite his poem. The entire class broke into a sigh followed by tears from every eye as Kirk placed the flowers on Becky's desk and proclaimed: "And my choice is you! Will you go with me?"

Becky's emotions would not allow her to answer at that time, so Kirk just asked her to think about it and then left. It is my understanding that the date was a complete success. Kirk took her out on the floor in her wheelchair and danced all around her as she danced within her chair. On the last dance of the evening he picked her up out of the chair and danced all around the dance floor with her cradled in his arms as she laughed and cried. I'll never forget her expression on the last day of class as we had a small testimony meeting. There Becky expressed thanks for that experience and said she could hardly wait for the resurrection, when she would be able to "dance and dance and dance."

The Lord can be a tremendous help in making decisions about love. When I had been home for six months from a mission I was visited by a girl I had dated at Ricks College and who had written me for two years while I was on my mission. Her visit threw me into a state of indecision about love. I had previously designed to tell the Lord of my decision to marry Monica and seek his confirmation, but procrastination had held me back. When Donna appeared on the scene both my logic and my emotions became confused, and I was beset with rationalizations. Donna was extremely attractive, and from everything apparent on the surface I felt she was spiritual and would make a good wife and mother. So after weighing things in my mind I decided that I would ask Donna to marry me.

On a clear California winter morning I went to a personal and sacred spot to tell the Lord of my decision. Upon kneeling down I told him why I was there and then said that I had chosen ". . . uh . . ." I could not remember her name! As hard as I concentrated, I could not remember Donna's name. It wasn't until I pulled her picture out of my wallet and looked at her signature on the back of it that I realized I had just experienced the biggest stupor of thought in my life.

I walked around the park for some two hours before returning to that spot and asking about Monica, at which time I knew what the mind and will of Father in Heaven was. The Lord knows the beginning and the end.

Being curious about love, I went to my ninety-six-year-old grandmother and asked her what she thought love was. She teared up as she said, "Being able to say 'I love you' every day and showing it by your actions and by praying together." Grandma had been without Grandpa for thirty-one years, but when I asked her if she loved him, with great emotion she said, "I love him much more today than the day he died, and I miss him so much!"

When I approached my other grandmother with similar questions, she told me about Grandpa at the time when he was in his seventies, when because of his injuries and operations he could not care for himself. Grandma bathed him, fed him, and carried him everywhere. He felt so embarrassed and sad and just wanted to die. On an earlier occasion Grandpa had asked Grandma if she loved him. She looked at him with those loving eyes and said: ''I love you, Elmer, and I married you for eternity. I will stick by you when you are old and when you are too sick to care for yourself, or when you are insane or not yourself. I will care for you.'' She did just that.

Well, Grandpa died, and at the age of eighty-seven Grandma married the most humorous, most loving man in all of Malad, Idaho. And we all witnessed love in old age. If love is such a young person's thing, how could two old wrinkled souls be so in love? They were the cutest couple as they marched in the parades as George and Martha Washington, and as they were seen snuggling and holding hands and doing things for each other. Mitchell even won the bid on the baby blanket, and when Grandma asked why he wanted it he replied, ''A man can be hopeful, can't he?''

A year and a half after their marriage Grandmother passed on to the spirit world. I was with her the day before her passing. On the morning that she passed away she told Mitchell that Elmer had visited her in the night and that he wanted her to come to be with him in the spirit world. She told Mitchell that she needed to go. Mitchell said he understood. Grandma asked Mitchell to lie on the hospital bed with her, so he climbed up on the bed and held her as they snuggled. She thanked him for the time together and kissed him good-bye, closed her eyes, and passed to the other side. Now when I think of love, I think of growing old in love and sharing a lifetime and an eternity with someone.

My deepest feelings about love have even changed during 1990. Sixteen years before, I had married Monica for eternity in the Los Angeles Temple. That day the Lord gave me an experience I will never forget. As I looked across the altar, her face became very clear and everything around her face was like a halo. I remember thinking, ''The Lord has given me an angel.'' The next sixteen years that followed were like a fairy-tale, with dreams and travel and children and love and the gospel. I can't remember a day without prayer and the expression of love and excitement. We became best friends. Each year was better and each year we found ourselves more in love.

In the late summer of 1990 my beloved Monica was suddenly taken to the spirit world through a car accident. I know now what Grandma was saying when she said she loved Grandpa more now than the day he died, for I know that that love swells within me as I think about spending the eternities with someone I love more than life itself.

May we all be found following the living prophet as we consider the true meaning of love as we see things for what they really are and what they should be.

Mark A. Bybee, a seminary teacher in Hyrum, Utah, holds a master's degree in Recreational Management. He enjoys racquetball, the martial arts, outdoor recreation generally, and high-risk sports such as kayaking and white water rafting. He encourages young people to "look forward," and "look to the Savior for help." Mark and his wife, Lisa, have six children.

9

Controlling Unworthy Thoughts

Brad Wilcox

"Could I . . . uh . . ." The dark-haired young man in front of me shifted awkwardly. "I mean, I was wondering . . . if we could talk." I had just finished speaking at a fireside for young people.

"No problem," I assured him. We walked down the meeting-house hall, away from the groups of people still lingering and enjoying refreshments. I had noticed this particular young man during the fireside. He was tall, handsome, and so clean-cut that he looked as if he could be on the cover of the *New Era.*

"It's about what you said in there," he began quietly. "You know, about being worthy. Well . . ." He hesitated. "Well . . . I . . ." He paused again. His averted eyes did little to disguise the tears that were welling. "It's my thoughts." He forced the words out. "Sometimes I just have the worst thoughts. It's my biggest problem." He shrugged his shoulders and sighed. "I don't know. Sometimes, I just feel so . . . so . . ."

"Dirty?" I filled in his blank. He nodded. The tears glistening on his lashes brimmed over.

In the minutes that followed we talked privately and my new friend asked several questions. The first was, "Am I normal?"

Inappropriate thoughts are a natural part of being human and a very normal part of growing up. At one time or another we have all felt a little hypocritical because we know that the thoughts found in our heads are not found in the Family Home Evening manual. At times, many of us have felt that we should "be glad if we could command the rocks and the mountains to fall upon us to hide us" (Alma 12:14) because of our thoughts. We might not even be seeing the movies that are for "mature" audiences, yet at times we're sure that there is an international film festival going on in our heads! We feel embarrassed. We feel weak, small, unworthy, and, like my new friend who came to me after the fireside, we feel a little dirty.

In the *New Era* we read, "You are not morally sick just because bad thoughts sometimes come into your mind. Thoughts are powerful, and all of us at times have trouble dealing with them" (May 1989, p. 17).

My friend's next question went something like this: "If I really don't want them, where do evil thoughts come from?" He's right. We don't want evil thoughts. Not many people I know wake up in the morning saying, "My, I wonder what dirty thoughts I'll have today." The thoughts just come without being invited—that's part of the problem.

We see an attractive person of the opposite sex and bells ring inside our heads. We see shorts that are too short and—as sure as Pavlov's dogs—we hear those bells. We hear people tell off-color jokes or twist an innocent phrase to mean something totally unintended, and the bells ring. Then the same jokes replay themselves over and over in our minds and it's as if someone has a finger on the doorbell button and is not letting up. I have even read a few choice words here and there on the walls of public rest rooms and have walked away thinking, "Well, I've never really seen it put quite like that before!"

Unbidden thoughts and ideas seem to demand room in our heads even when we have placed the No Vacancy sign in clear view. Like red traffic lights when we're late to church, those thoughts are simply a part of everyday living in this telestial world. President Ezra Taft Benson assures us, "Our accountability begins with how we handle the evil thought immediately *after* it is presented" (*Ensign*, March 1989, p. 4, italics added).

"Then"—my friend asked his next question—"are my evil thoughts sins?" It is an important question. The Savior warned, "Whosoever looketh on a woman to lust after her hath committed adultery with her already *in his heart*" (Matthew 5:28, italics added). In Proverbs we read, "As [a man] thinketh *in his heart* so is he" (Proverbs 23:7, italics added). Truman G. Madsen writes: "Reread the oft-quoted passages about the thoughts. You will note that it is not the occurrence of ideas in the head but their lodgment in the heart that degrades. . . . The issue is not so much what thoughts occur in our minds, but how we nurture them in our desires." (*Christ and the Inner Life* [Salt Lake City: Bookcraft, 1978], p. 35.)

Our minds are like rivers, and unworthy thoughts are like birds that swoop down out of nowhere to snatch an unsuspecting fish. If we do all we can to get rid of the pesky birds rapidly, the river has not been blocked or slowed. There has been nothing more than a mere splash on the surface of our minds. Such disturbances happen to everyone and are in no way sins.

However, inviting the birds down and coaxing them out of the sky is a different story. If we allow those visiting birds to sit on the water and let them dip deeper and deeper in the river for bigger and bigger fish, then the birds will ultimately create a dam, so to speak, in our river. Our progress will be slowed and diverted. Such blockage indicates a sin that requires repentance.

We read in the scriptures that the disobedient "shall be damned" (D&C 42:60). Now and then someone will even quote one such forceful passage over the pulpit (much to the delight of all the snickering deacons in the front two rows at the side of the chapel). We hear the word *damned*, which means "condemned," but doctrinally it translates also into the meaning of the similar word *dammed*, which signifies "stopped up" or "blocked." This is a literal, wonderful description of the effects of sin in our lives. Sin blocks our progress. It most literally dams us, keeps us from moving forward in the course God wills us to follow.

So, are my thoughts sins? I can check myself by asking: "Are these thoughts blocking my progress? Are they keeping me from my worthy goals? Are they slowing me in any way?" If the honest answer is yes, then, my thoughts have become sins because I have allowed them to sink below the surface of my mind into my heart. If I do not repent and change, then I am, most definitely, "damned."

My friend Clark Smith says, "You might not be able to keep a bird from landing on your head but you *can* keep him from building a nest there!" Perhaps we can say that we might not be able to keep a bird from landing on our river ("Whosoever *looketh* on a woman") but we *can* keep him from building a multi-million dollar hydroelectric dam ("to *lust* after her").

My new friend had only one question more: "Since I can't really stop the birds from landing, how do I get rid of them quickly? How do I control unworthy thoughts?" Elder Robert E. Wells has written, "Self-control will lead to Christ, but that means giving up the things of the world and changing our thoughts" (*The Mount and the Master* [Salt Lake City: Deseret Book Company, 1991], p. xiii). Brigham Young said, "The greatest mystery a man ever learned is to know how to control the human mind" (*Journal of Discourses* 1:46).

Following are some of the ideas I shared with my friend. Perhaps one or two might be helpful for you as well.

Replace wrong thoughts with right ones. Most of us have heard that we should sing a hymn when we have evil thoughts. The only problem I've ever had with this advice is that I like to sing. I'll burst out in song just for fun, and you would be amazed at the astonished looks I get from those around me who are sure I need to reread *The Miracle of Forgiveness.*

I remember an occasion during my mission in Chile when my companion and I had to walk by a typical South American beach. I told my companion, "Elder, sing a hymn!" He obediently started singing, "There is beauty all around."

One young woman went to her bishop about the problem of inappropriate thoughts. He said, "Think of a hymn." She responded: "But, Bishop, that's the problem. I can't *stop* thinking of *him.*"

Elder Boyd K. Packer's principle is sound: We get rid of unworthy thoughts by replacing them with worthy ones. As with digging a hole in the back yard, if I don't want the dirt to just get pushed back in when the next rainstorm comes, I had better put something else—like cement—in place of the dirt.

Remove stumbling blocks. We're all familiar with the advice given in Matthew 5:30—"If thy right hand offend thee, cut it off"—yet too many are unclear as to what it really means. Todd Parker teaches: "A better definition of the word *offend* from the original Greek is 'cause to stumble.' In other words, if your . . . hand is tempted to touch something that would cause you to stumble spiritually, the Savior's advice is to get rid of the temptation. You should get away from it or not get near whatever it is that tempts you. He is suggesting that not only do we *not* do the sin, but also that we not even get near the temptation, let alone the sin." (*High Fives and High Hopes* [Salt Lake City: Deseret Book Co., 1990], p. 96.)

Working on Sunday, swearing, listening to inappropriate music, viewing pornography, seeing R-rated movies—*any* R-rated movies—hanging around with friends who are bad influences, dating before sixteen and then pairing up and steady dating having reached sixteen—these are all activities that can feed inappropriate thought birds. Let's do as we are counseled by the Savior and cut out of our lives any activities that are causing us to stumble.

Change environments. Sometimes, when we find ourselves in places where lights are low and thoughts are even lower, we must simply get out. Change environments. Just as sure as Joseph did of old (see Genesis 39:12), sometimes we just have to run away.

At Especially for Youth a young man came up to me and said, "Brother Wilcox, I know exactly what you mean!" It seems that a certain young lady in his home ward came over to his house to listen to music. His stereo happened to be downstairs in his bedroom, and as they sat on his bed listening, the girl said, "Turn over and I'll give you a back rub."

This young man said to me, "I knew I really shouldn't, but, Brother Wilcox—it felt so good."

After a while, the girl said, "Take off your shirt and I'll rub you with some lotion."

"I knew I shouldn't," came the response again, "but, Brother Wilcox . . ." Suddenly the girl started taking off *her* shirt. The boy told me: "I didn't know what to do. I didn't want to look stupid and I didn't want her to think I was weird, but I just said, 'Hey, you want to listen to music? You listen to the music. I'm getting out of here!' " And he ran. Bless him—he ran out of his own house.

Do something active. We are all well aware of the connection between our brains and our bodies. We can all name people who simply could not talk if their hands were tied behind them. However, we do not use this interconnection to our advantage as often as we should. Just as the mind can affect body movement, body movement can affect the mind.

Most of you can remember talking with someone (or speaking at the pulpit in sacrament meeting) when suddenly your mind went completely blank. You were right in the middle of a sentence, but then you could no more remember what you had just been thinking than you could quote 2 Nephi by heart.

When your mind goes blank like that, chances are you have moved your body. That simple movement totally erased a thought. So when we *want* our minds to go blank, let's move.

"Oh, sure," some might be thinking, "jumping jacks in the middle of biology class." Not necessarily. Just try crossing arms, legs, ankles, fingers, and then uncross them and do it again. Move your hands. Wiggle your toes. It sounds strange, but when someone asks you what on earth you're doing you might not remember, and that's the whole idea.

Do "all that stuff." My second grade daughter calls it "all that stuff." We were having family night and I asked, "What can we do to be happy?" After a long pause she exhaled loudly, rolled her eyes dramatically, and sighed, "Just . . . just do . . . all that stuff!" The more I think about it, she's absolutely right.

By "all that stuff" she meant to pray; read the scriptures, the *New Era,* and Church books; participate in Young Men or Young Women activities and service projects; attend Church meetings; get close to leaders; request regular interviews with your bishop; fellowship those who are less active, be trustworthy, loyal, helpful, friendly, courteous, kind. . . . The list of constructive activities with which to occupy our minds and our time is endless.

One recently baptized young man was asked whether joining the Church had solved all his problems. He smiled: "No, but it has left me with a lot less time to worry about them." When we're dealing with the problem of unworthy thoughts, we need to remember that the less time we give Satan the less trouble he will be able to give us. "Commit thy works unto the Lord," we are instructed, "and thy thoughts shall be established" (Proverbs 16:3).

Celebrate private victories. When you mow the lawn or do homework, people say, "Wonderful!" If you lose twenty pounds, people say, "Outstanding!" When you get your Duty to God or Young Women recognition award, everyone says, "Excellent!" When I'm really trying to go the extra mile, John Bytheway even says to me, "Thou art cool!"

But what happens when we control our thoughts? Do parents say, "Sweetheart, we know that myriad triple X-rated grossities and impurities are spawning in your mind and you're controlling them. We are so proud of you!" No way! There is no space on the school report card for an A+ in thought control. When I cast out an improper thought, no one really knows except God and me. So it is up to the two of us to throw the party!

Once I was waiting for a plane in an airport in southern California. I was just sitting there writing in my journal when suddenly a man came over, sat down right next to me, and proceeded to unfold a magazine in plain view—and it was *not* the *Ensign!*

I buried my head in my journal. My writing started looking shaky. The sentences were going all over the page, but I just kept writing: "I will not look up. I will not even think about looking up. I will absolutely, definitely not look up."

Now I open my journal to that particular page with a lot of laughs and a great deal of personal pride. It was a victory—a private victory but nonetheless a victory. I celebrated as if my school had just taken state! I praised myself and rewarded myself. I remember the peace that Heavenly Father sent on that occasion—the peace that is promised in Mosiah 4. I felt it. I loved it. I let it reinforce me, and it encouraged me to make the same positive choice again in the future. I was better for having taken a moment to celebrate my private victory.

Be with others. Stay with groups. Be with good friends. Include family. Many young people tell me that when they are at Especially for Youth, a youth conference, or seminary, they never have problems with their thoughts. Why? Besides being positive spiritual environments, these activities also involve groups of people. A mind that is focused on others has a hard time focusing on selfish desires. Staying with other people keeps you from being alone with your thoughts.

Obviously, there are times when we have to be alone. We can't bring everyone at EFY over to watch us go to sleep every night or get ready in the morning. If those are times when unworthy thoughts creep in, leave your bedroom door ajar or the bathroom door unlocked. That small effort to open yourself to others will leave you feeling much less secure and comfortable in personal moments. Believe me, the fact that someone else could, might, and probably will come in at any time is enough to keep you on track. Knowing that you could at any minute be entertaining a little brother or sister might just be enough to keep you from entertaining temptation.

Understand dreams. Perhaps dreams are the most misunderstood realm of thought. Now and then, most of us feel a little shocked by what we dream. On those mornings, the best thing to do is simply let it go. Forget the dream and move on.

Our dreams are classical, respondent behavior, controlled completely by preceding stimuli—much like the constriction of the pupils of our eyes when someone shines a flashlight at them. Given the bright light, we cannot consciously will our pupils not to constrict. In the same way, we cannot consciously control our dreams; and thus we cannot be held accountable for them and should not feel so bad about them. Let dreams go. It's O.K. to leave the night behind and begin the day in peace.

If dreams become a major problem, rather than focusing on what is coming out of your mind at night zero in on what is being allowed into your mind during the day—especially right before bed. If I don't want constricted pupils, I'd better not let anyone with a flashlight even close to my eye.

Remember the Savior. All of us have made covenants to remember Christ always (see D&C 20:77,79). What better time to remember him than when we are having unworthy thoughts? Truman G. Madsen suggests: "Picture Christ and remember how you are bound to him. In the crisis, for example, when your temples thunder, imagine what you are tempted to do as if it were a large sledge hammer. See! See if you can stand at the cross and by this act or indulgence swing that hammer on the nail. That will break your compulsive pattern and restore enough to your consciousness to enable you to cry out and *mean, 'No!' " (Christ and the Inner Life,* p. 37.)

In the Doctrine and Covenants the Lord tells us, "Look unto me in every thought" (D&C 6:36). Elder Robert E. Wells teaches that the true key to becoming a disciple of Christ is to fill your mind with thoughts of the Savior, fill your heart with love of the Savior, and fill your life with service. "Through following these paths," writes Elder Wells, "bad men become good and good men become better; the sinner becomes a saint." (*We Are Christians Because* . . . [Salt Lake City: Deseret Book Company, 1985], p. 108.)

Request a special blessing. Ask for a blessing from your father or a priesthood leader. Just as Christ blessed eyes to see and ears to hear, I believe that minds can be blessed to think on higher levels.

"Oh, sure," some might say, "I'm going to just run up to my dad and ask him to bless me to get my brain out of the gutter." Dads and priesthood leaders understand much more than we might think they will. However, if you feel uncomfortable you do not need to tell anyone the specific reason why you are requesting a blessing, for a sensitive priesthood holder will simply take his place as a mouthpiece. You will receive your special blessing and counsel from our all-seeing Heavenly Father, who understands completely, in the name of Jesus Christ, who knows exactly how you feel—not in some mythical Santa-knows-whether-you-have-been-naughty-or-nice way, but rather because he has been there.

"Are any of our conceivable evil thoughts beyond the Lord? If so, would there be any sound foundation for trust in him? . . .

". . . How low then can we go in our thoughts? Not as low as he in the contemplation of evil. He was tempted through 'the darkest abyss' and 'descended below all things.' Why? That he might be 'in and through *all* things the light of truth.' What? In and through *my* vagrant, aching, turbulent, unworthy thoughts? 'Yes. . . .' He has comprehended them all. His is the compassion of kinship. (D&C 88:6.)" (Truman G. Madsen, *Christ and the Inner Life*, pp. 34–35.)

Think it through to the end. After we have tried to cast out evil thoughts and they still linger, perhaps we need to try a different approach. Rather than thinking so hard about not thinking, try instead taking the time to think—really think. And, more important, think beyond.

If I take time to analyze each little detail of a passionate fantasy, I must also take time to think of the other moments that are sure to follow—not fantasies at all. I must think of the guilt that will be felt by my spirit as surely as pain is felt by my body. I must picture having to face people the following day and imagine looking in my own mirror. I must ponder about having to tell parents and a bishop. Further, I must think thirty years down the road, when I'll be bringing my children to Temple Square for general conference and there maybe running into a certain person from the past who is also visiting. How will I feel when I end up in a situation in which I might actually have to introduce my children to that person?

Everyone loves fireworks on the Fourth of July, but few consider that on the fifth of July someone has to clean up the mess. Elder M. Russell Ballard explains: ''One of Satan's clever tactics is to tempt us to concentrate on the present and ignore the future. . . . We must govern our actions every day with our future in mind.'' (*Ensign*, November 1990, p. 36.)

Keep perspective. ''The Lord gives us the feelings of love and attraction, strong bonds that he wants us to use as the center of a united, eternal family. What you must do is learn to channel those feelings in the right direction, to understand them as part of the process of growing and learning, of preparing for a temple marriage, leading someday to family life in a celestial realm.'' (*New Era*, May 1989, p. 18.)

Many of the same thoughts that are carelessly referred to as ''bad'' will someday, in the right place, at the right time, with the right person, be very good. Remember, passions are not meant to be eliminated, expelled, and cut out of our lives forever. They are to be bridled (see Alma 38:12). Appetites are not to be removed but to be regulated. Desires are not to be ruled out but to be ruled. Thoughts are not to be conquered but to be controlled.

''It's my thoughts.'' That's what my dark-haired friend said to me after the fireside. ''Sometimes I just have the worst thoughts.'' I hope he now knows that he is not alone. I hope he knows that lots of people understand and care. Most of all, I hope he knows that he can control unworthy thoughts. We all can. It is important. It is possible. With Heavenly Father's help, all of us can ''let virtue garnish [our] thoughts unceasingly'' so that our ''confidence [will] wax strong in the presence of God'' (D&C 121:45).

Brad Wilcox, a teacher on the Elementary Education faculty at BYU, spent his childhood years in Ethiopia and has traveled all over the world. He enjoys writing Church magazine articles, reading his kids bedtime stories, journal writing, and watching videos of classic movies. Two favorite former assignments are sixth-grade teacher and Primary chorister. Brad and his wife, Debi, have three children.

10

Making Positive Changes

Barbara Barrington Jones

After speaking at a youth conference in Texas, I received the following letter from one young man:

Dear Sister Jones:

Hi! How are you? You probably don't remember me at all, but I just *had* to write. I was at youth conference. . . . I wish I knew what to say to you. . . . There really aren't words to explain how everything is changing for me.

Before I went to youth conference, I was seriously thinking about suicide. I admit that something had to have been wrong with my head. It was probably a loose screw. I was unpopular in school, ate lunch all alone, and was a little "chunky." I also felt very depressed and unloved.

Well, after youth conference, I decided to get rid of the sad, depressed me. I lost fifteen pounds, got a job, and bought some cool-looking clothes and made some "new" friends.

My new friends were a great help. They helped me gradually change myself. Now, the new me is active in school and got a lead part in a musical play. I feel like a fifty-pound jacket has been lifted off my back. People who wouldn't look at me last year are now coming up to me excitedly telling me things like, "There's going to be a party at so-and-so's house." It's great. I feel like that loose screw has been tightened up. I feel like that coat has been taken off and burned. My parents trust me more now. They aren't worried about me and they like my friends too.

Well, what can I say? Thanks!

> Your new friend,
> Michael

After reading that letter, I was so proud of this young man. He has made some positive changes in his life. I read his letter over and over and analyzed it. Michael has done things right. I believe we can all learn from his example.

In his letter Michael said, "I decided." That is the first step. Michael said he was unpopular, overweight, sad, and depressed. But *he decided* to change. He didn't sit around saying, "Boy, if only I could lose fifteen pounds, then my life would be great." He said, "I decided to lose fifteen pounds." And he did it.

Remember when you were a kid? Your mother said, "You are going to eat your spinach."

You thought to yourself, That's what you think, Mom.

She said, "Eat your spinach."

You said, "No, thank you."

She started calling you by your full given name complete with initials and said, "You *will* eat your spinach."

You thought, I will *not* eat this spinach. You made up your mind, and neither bribe nor threat made any difference to you. The whole BYU defensive line couldn't have got that spinach in your mouth. That's the same determination Michael showed when he decided to lose weight.

Next, after really deciding to change, Michael had to be willing to pay the price; he had to work to realize his goal. In his letter, Michael wrote, "I got a job and bought some cool-looking clothes." He didn't say. "I sure wish I had some cool clothes." He made a plan, found a part-time job, and earned the money he needed. He decided and he worked.

Regardless of what many in the world would have us believe, there are no easy ways or short cuts. There are no "free lunches" when it comes to positive self-improvement.

I have an uncle who lives in Clint, Texas. He's always doing silly things for me. For example, once he sent me a cassette tape of his pet canary, Spot. Yes, the bird was named Spot. I clicked the tape into my tape player and punched the button. It was an hour and a half of the chirping of my uncle's bird. I couldn't believe it.

Recently I had the chance to visit that uncle. He greeted me at the door wearing coveralls and a floppy hat; and, just like in the movies, he had a piece of straw hanging out of his mouth. He said, "Barbara, come on in here and sit yourself down. You have got to hear a cassette tape I have."

I thought, Great, another ninety minutes of Spot chirping. My uncle then played a cassette he had made of a radio commercial: "Ladies over one thousand pounds, are you fat? Are you taller lying down than standing up? On hot days, do people gather on your shady side? When you come on the scene, does the scene disappear? Is your dress size junior missile? Were you born on the eighth, ninth, and tenth of March? When you step on the dog's tail, do they have to call him Beaver? When you sit down, is the person sitting next to you, you? When the local elementary school wanted to adopt a whale to save, did they call your number? If so, you need the amazing new Flab-Off. It's not a liquid or a salve, but a five-pound pill. Be sure to order your free cramming rods so you can get it down. Just send $4.98. Act now!"

I laughed till I could hardly breathe. My uncle just smiled. I played the tape again and wrote down every word. I read it in one of my classes at Especially for Youth. That's when the laughing stopped. After the class, one girl came up privately and asked seriously, "Where do I send for those diet pills?"

This young sister and I had a long talk about free lunches. I told her: "I'm afraid there are no magic pills and no easy ways. If you really want to lose a little weight or obtain any worthy goal, you must be willing to work."

One young man I met admitted that he had to learn this lesson too. One day when he was about twelve he passed his mother an envelope and twenty-five dollars as he ran out of the door. "Will you mail that for me?" he called to her.

Inside the envelope was a coupon which read, "Just send twenty-five dollars and we'll send you this amazing cream that will give you muscles overnight. All you have to do is rub a little of this on your upper arms and voila!" Needless to say, his mom did not send the twenty-five dollars.

We all see similar advertisements in newspapers and magazines.

"Watch your eyelashes grow overnight."

"For longer, thicker hair, send $7.95."

"The Scandinavian Fat Blocker—eat and still lose weight. No diet, no exercise, awesome new discovery. Easy and automatic. No effort. Now you can have what you have always dreamed of. Money-back guarantee."

My favorite was one I saw recently that said, "Read this only if you want money—lots of money." It was pushing a good luck charm.

At times all of us wish we could send off for pills, creams, and charms that would change everything bad in our lives. But it is not that simple. If something sounds too easy and effortless to be true, it probably is.

The price we have to pay to reach our positive goals has very little to do with money. We must be willing to do exactly what Michael did—sacrifice and work hard to obtain the results we're after.

Some might be thinking, "But there are some bad things in my life that I just couldn't ever change, as hard as I might try." Remember Michael's letter—"I decided to get rid of the sad, depressed me." Michael had the courage to overcome a negative attitude.

Satan loves to get us feeling sorry for ourselves. He came to Christ with the word *if* (see Matthew 4). He comes to us with the words *if only.*

"If only I looked like Susan . . . If only I had straight hair . . . If only I were shorter . . . If only I were taller . . . If only I had a better family . . . If only my parents weren't divorced . . . If only my father were active . . . If only my parents believed I am as good as my brother . . ." The list goes on and on.

Often we find ourselves in imperfect circumstances that are totally beyond our control. However, like Michael, one thing we always have complete control over is our attitude.

When my husband, Hal, and I were first married, he said: "There's eighty percent of me that's good and there's twenty percent of me that is not so good. If you choose to look at my eighty percent, we are going to be happy. If you choose to look at my twenty percent, our marriage isn't going to be all that great." So it is with many things in our lives.

Most parents have eighty percent that is good and twenty percent that's not so good. The same is true of brothers, sisters, school, work, and even many of the experiences we have in church. It is up to us to decide which part to look at—the eighty or the twenty. In any person or situation, we can choose to dwell either on the negative or the positive. And just as my husband says, we can all find greater happiness if we look for the eighty.

My daughter, Wendy, who is now putting in her papers for her mission, had a rough junior year in high school. Looking back on it she says, "Mom, it was all because of my own attitude."

I remember taking her to a beauty shop before school started, because she wanted a new hair style. When the cut was done, Wendy turned to me with tears in her eyes and cried: "I hate it! You've ruined me!"

After the first day of school, I picked Wendy up. Before she even got in the car she said: "Mom, this is going to be the worst year of my entire life. Do you know who I got for my classes? Do you know who's in my classes?" She then complained about each teacher and student throughout her entire schedule.

I thought, In a few days this will all blow over. I was wrong. You see, Wendy liked one guy, but he never asked her out. Then another guy started asking her out, and he was okay but he wasn't as good as the first guy. When Christmas came, neither guy asked her to the formal because they both thought the other one already had. Wendy didn't get to go at all. "I told you this would be the worst year," she sobbed.

I said, "Wendy, look for the eighty percent."

"You sound just like Dad!" she wailed.

Soon after this, Wendy's good friends Jason and Andy were traveling to a game where Wendy was cheer leading. They were involved in a terrible car accident and were both killed. "It was a horrible accident" the papers reported. "It's so sad" teachers and friends said. "It should never have happened" was the comment heard over and over at school. But, like many difficult and trying circumstances of life, it did happen. None of us had control over that. We couldn't change it.

Wendy was devastated by the deaths. She was upset and angry. She was mad at the situation and the world; and deep down, she was mad at God. Rather than lifting an open hand upward for Heavenly Father's help when she needed it most, Wendy chose instead to raise a fist.

As the year came to an end, Wendy decided, at her Dad's suggestion, that it would be healthy to get away. She signed up with Teen Missions International, a youth service group that was going to New Guinea to do work projects for the needy.

After two days of training, Wendy and her group flew to Australia and then to New Guinea. There they were loaded in the back of trucks and driven for forty-eight hours to the edge of a river. The group was then put in canoes for an eighteen-hour trip to the village where they would live. By that time these young people were exhausted. They had jet lag, truck lag, and canoe lag. They wanted to crash in bed and sleep, but the only thing they were given were sleeping bags and tents.

Most of the time, it was pouring with rain. It was also very hot —one hundred twenty degrees, to be exact. The only type of shoes that the young people could bring were a pair of work boots, and in the weeks that followed, those boots were worn out completely.

Wendy's work team built a hospital and a bridge. They had no machinery, so everything had to be done by hand. Wendy worked harder than she ever had. The team awoke early and rarely even stopped for a rest during the day. They couldn't. If they didn't get their part of the construction done on time it would hold up other groups.

Wendy recalls: "At night I wanted to cry, but no tears ever came. I had blisters that were sore and broken. My back hurt and my muscles ached. I wanted to cry, but it was too hard." So it went, day after day, until one afternoon, while timbers for the bridge were being moved, an accident occurred. A huge log fell and crushed the hand of one of the team members. The girl screamed in pain. Blood was everywhere.

Quickly the group gathered around and hoisted the heavy wood off their friend's hand. Adult supervisors called on short-wave radio for a helicopter to come, and the injured girl was flown out for medical help.

The teenagers who remained behind were tired. These young people were sore, dirty, and covered with sweat. They could have said: "This is stupid! We want to go home. If we weren't here in this awful place, this accident never would have happened." The teenagers could have complained loud and long about their supervisors, their companions, and their horrible accommodations. They could have said, "This has been the worst experience of our lives."

However, these teenagers chose a different course. They looked for the eighty. In their anxiety and total helplessness, these teenagers did not gripe and whine. Rather, they knelt in prayer. They prayed over and over into the night.

Finally, at 3:00 a.m., the team got a call that their friend would be O.K. In fact, not one bone in the girl's hand had been broken.

Wendy says: "That's when I cried—not because of my troubles and problems, but out of gratitude." Yes, this time there were tears—not of self-pity but of appreciation. Prayers had been answered. Lives had been changed. Wendy felt as if she had witnessed a miracle.

When my daughter finally came home I was waiting as she got off the plane. She looked like a native of New Guinea. She had on a long muumuu and was even carrying spears. She was tanned and exhausted, but she was smiling and laughing. Handing her spears to one of her teammates, and signaling for me to wait, she whipped off her muumuu. Underneath, she had on a nice skirt and top that she had bought in Australia. She looked fantastic. She was healthy, in shape, and feeling great.

I asked, "What do you want to do first?"

"I want to take a real bath," she answered. When we got home and Wendy turned on the water she exclaimed, "Look, Mom, running water!" In the days that followed, Wendy couldn't stop counting her blessings. Suddenly she was seeing all the good things in her life. She had gained a testimony that God lives, loves us, and really is there for us—even during hard times. Wendy looked for the eighty and, at last, she found it.

At the start of her senior year, Wendy went to the hair dresser —the same one she had gone to the previous year. After the cut, Wendy looked in the mirror and said: "I love it. I just love it, and I love you too!" The hairdresser almost fainted. My daughter had a wonderful senior year. The teachers were the same as the year before. The students were the same. The school had not really changed at all. But—and here's the point—Wendy's attitude had.

Michael said in his letter, "There really aren't words to explain how everything is changing for me." That is exactly how each one of us can feel if we will do what Michael did. We must decide to change. We must sacrifice and work without looking for an easy way or a free lunch. Finally, when there are things we cannot change, we must keep a positive attitude and look for the eighty. Then, just like Michael, all of us can feel as if those loose screws have been tightened up and those heavy-coat burdens have been lifted. Then all of us can approach our Heavenly Father humbly and say: "Well, what can I say? Thanks."

Barbara Barrington Jones, an image consultant, grooms young women for beauty pageants. She likes walking, healthy foods, working with youth, and writing books. A world traveler, she has been a fashion designer/coordinator, modeling school owner, and classical ballet dancer. She says, "The greatest event in my life was finding Christ in this Church." Barbara and her husband, Hal, have two children.

11

Attitude: A Totally Terrific Idea to Undermine Decreased Esteem

Stephen Jason Hall

On July 13, 1986, I was vacationing with my family at Lake Powell, Utah. On the day we arrived I skied all day long. I went to sleep that night and awoke the next day to a beautiful Lake Powell sunrise. As the sun shone over the horizon it warmed my entire body, beginning with my face and working its way down. It was one of those "It's great to be alive" mornings. I got up and made ready for the day's activities.

One of the kids suggested that we go to Moki Canyon, so we all jumped in our boats and did just that. And when I say all, I mean *all*. On this vacation there were eight LDS families, which meant *jillions* of kids. The parents drove in cars, and the kids followed in "Ryder" trucks. As we reached the canyon I looked up and noticed the high, sheer cliffs nature had cut from the red sandstone.

In the center of the canyon was a big sand dune. One of the kids explained that the object of the game was to run down the dune and jump, dive, flip, or whatever into the water. Everybody excitedly ran up the hill—that is, everybody but my cousin, David, his girlfriend, and myself. We had decided to just stay at the bottom and build a sand castle, because David's girlfriend was scared that he would get hurt. And since I loved being with David more than I loved running down sand dunes, I decided to stay.

After stopping half-way up to rest, the group resumed the ascent. Two of them, my cousin and her friend, turned round, and with all their teenage charm and female finesse, called out to me,

"Jason, come on up." I thought to myself: Two beautiful babes in swimsuits! Like, I'm going to tell them no! I mean, I was fifteen years old, a walking hormone. And I didn't love David *that* much. So I ran up the hill after these two girls.

Just as I reached the top, one of the kids cried, "One, two, three, go," and everyone started running *down* the hill. I was bushed, but I hadn't run all the way up the hill alone just to run down in the same condition; so, as tired as I was, I followed. I was a couple of feet behind the group, getting sand kicked in my eyes, my feet aching and burning from the hot sand. My fifteen-year-old brain said, If this is what dating's like, count me out! As I reached the water, I felt it come up to my ankles and then to my knees. Then I dived.

When I dived, I heard an incredibly loud crack that began in my neck and resonated throughout my entire body. The next thing I knew, I was in the depths of that big lake, totally and completely helpless. I did my best to keep afloat, banging my arms against the water, but to no avail. I saw the water over my head and felt myself sinking deeper and deeper to the bottom of the lake.

It was then that the Lord brought about a miracle on my behalf. My body actually came out of the water up to my chest, with my arm outstretched straight up in the air. My sister saw me — saw the terror on my face, knew that I was in trouble, and screamed for help. I went straight down back into the water. But some of the kids ran over, grabbed me, and pulled me out onto the safety of the beach.

Now, to you this may not seem much of a miracle. But consider that even today, with all the strengthening that has taken place, when I lift my hand up in the air it simply falls as it approaches my head. My paralysis caused me to lose the use of my triceps. If you were to throw me into a swimming pool without a life jacket I would simply sink to the bottom and hang out near the drain until I ran out of breath. Some people call it drowning. I call it swimming. It's all in your perspective, right?

My dad ran across the beach to me, I looked him in the eyes and said, "Dad, I've been seriously injured. Can you please give me a blessing." He laid his hands on my head. I don't remember what he said and I don't remember how he said it, but what I do remember is this: Before he put his hands on my head I was as scared as I have ever been in my entire life. For the first time I had looked down at my feet and I no longer knew they were mine; I didn't know what to think and I didn't know what to do. But when my dad's hands left my head I felt calm and peaceful and I knew that everything was going to be O.K. I didn't know how I knew and I didn't know why I knew. I simply knew.

I have learned that the power of the priesthood is a wonderful blessing in the life of each of us, though sometimes we take it for granted. Probably there has been a time in your life when you felt, "I need a priesthood blessing," yet you didn't want to ask anyone because you didn't want to make a big deal about that feeling of need. You didn't want to "bother" your Heavenly Father with it, and you didn't want to "bother" your dad. But my experiences have taught me that we shouldn't feel that way, that we should not be reluctant to ask a worthy priesthood holder for a blessing of healing, help, strength, or comfort. Obviously, the need we have for such blessings is one of the reasons why the Lord put this power here on earth. If we will ask for the Lord's help in the form of a blessing, he will send his power through his servants and help us. I know this as surely as I know anything.

As I lay on the beach that morning I did all I could to stay positive. I sang the song "Count Your Blessings" over and over in my mind. You see, as I reflected on my blessings the day didn't seem as dismal, nor the night as dark. Soon the boat came that took me to a helipad, where I was put on a helicopter and flown to Grand Junction, Colorado. There I was rushed into the emergency room and to the cold metal slab that some people call an examination table. The doctor administered some tests and concluded that I had broken my neck at the fifth and sixth vertebrae; therefore, it was important that my neck be stabilized with traction. This was to be a most painful experience, and I prayed and prayed that the Lord would help me to endure it. And he did. He heard my prayer, and took my pain.

As I think back to that experience I am reminded that Jesus Christ took on all our pains, also our sicknesses and our infirmities, that he might have mercy upon us. I was so thankful to know that Heavenly Father was mindful enough of me, as he is of us all, that he knew what I could and could not handle. This means that when an adversity comes into our life, with our potential and with the Lord's help we can handle that adversity. We need to remember that and let our adversities help us to grow, as they were surely meant to do.

Those early days slowly passed, and as they did I began to lose my ability to breathe. To remedy this, a tube hooked to a respirator was passed down my throat and into my lungs. Now I was doing O.K., especially with the constant strength and help of my parents.

I well remember the day when my dad came into my room and told me he was going to have to leave and go home. The hospital bills were really piling up, and he had to get back to work in order to keep his job. That seemed a pretty good line of logic to me, but I wasn't very excited about it because at this time in my life I lived for three things, the most important being the blessing my dad gave me every night. It seemed that I could live through the day—the pain, the physical therapy, and all I had to endure—if I knew that every night I would get that blessing from my dad.

The second thing I lived for was the letters I got from my friends each day. How thankful I am for friends! Sometimes we forget the great support group we have in the Church amongst our friends. All the letters were different in their words, but their message was the same: "Jason, we love you and know you can make it." How that made me want to fight! The third thing was that every day at two the "Addams Family" was on TV. Nobody messed with my "Addams Family."

But the time had come for Dad to leave, and I didn't know what I was going to do. I prayed that night that the Lord would prepare a way for me to have the nightly blessing I so desperately needed. It is amazing how the Lord does prepare the way for us. Since my dad had to go, a local stake patriarch was made aware of my situation and offered to come every night to perform the service. When Brother Ransenberger came in my room and looked into my eyes, I knew he had been sent by Heavenly Father to do this work, to give me this blessing. Some might think of this as coincidence or luck, but I knew better. I knew that my Father helped me that day.

Not long after this I was taken out of traction and put into a halo. Some days later they replaced my air-giving tube with a tracheotomy (a tube that is inserted directly through the throat and down into the lungs). Time soon passed and they finally said, "We are going to send you to Salt Lake."

I was excited to go. First of all I have relatives in Salt Lake City, and also I was going to be closer to my family in Boise, Idaho. But more important, my mom was going to see me onto the helicopter, and my dad was going to meet me at the helipad in Salt Lake.

They put me in the helicopter and I lay there flat on my back in the big halo. All I could see out of the window was clouds. As this became boring, I asked the nurse to tell me what she saw. She said things like, "We're going over the Wasatch Front." "I can see the University Hospital." "I see the helipad." I remember mouthing to her, "My dad, my dad, can you see my dad?" She looked at me and said, "Yes, I can see your dad." After we had landed they put me on the gurney and took me around the helipad. The paramedics asked me, "Can you breathe? Is everything O.K.?" I remember that my eyes were saturated with tears and that it took all my strength to say, "My dad, my dad, where is my dad?" I only wanted to have him near me; he was my strength, my rock. And how wonderful it felt when he looked over my bed, held me in his arms, and said, "Jason, I am here, and I love you so very much!"

Since then I've often reflected that most of us take our parents for granted. I love my dad and my mom so much. In this experience they have been with me every second, every step of the way, and in similar circumstances most parents would do the same. Yet how often do we tell our parents how much we love them? How many times are we too busy? How many times is it not cool? Telling family members that we love them is so important to relationships that we shouldn't ever let an opportunity pass by.

I relate this whole experience of mine to what it might be like after death, when we go to heaven and perhaps are there walking around, saying, "My Father, my Father, where is my Father?" And probably we can't even imagine what it might feel like as we come into his presence, as he encircles us in his arms of love and says gently, as only a loving father can, "I am here, and I love you so very much." Nothing we could do in mortality—no combination of the "pleasurable" sins such as dishonesty, breaking the Word of Wisdom, sexual immorality—nothing could be worth the sacrifice of that moment, to say nothing of an eternity to be spent thereafter in Heavenly Father's presence. The recollection of my earthly father's welcome at the hospital prompts these reflections.

As I entered the critical care unit at the University of Utah Hospital in Salt Lake City, I was a little leery; first, of being in any way associated with the U of U (being a BYU Cougar fan from birth), and second, not being used to my new surroundings. I was to be initiated soon . . . too soon.

I recall lying in my room one night in critical care wanting a blanket for my cold legs. Quadriplegics feel as if everything is there. When you break your neck it doesn't feel as if you are two arms and a head floating all over the place. Just because you don't feel anything to the touch doesn't mean it feels that everything is gone. And sometimes your body feels cold, and sometimes it feels hot.

This night, whether it had a mental or a physical cause, my legs were cold, so I reached for my buzzer and called the nurse. When she came in I said, "My legs are cold." She felt my legs and then said, "Your legs aren't cold," and she left. I knew full well that my legs were cold, so I called her again. She came back in and said, "What?" I exclaimed, "My legs are cold." She said, "Your legs aren't cold," and she left again. I thought to myself, "We're paying four hundred dollars a night to stay here. I should take the money, rent a nurse, and go to the Hilton. The service would be better, and so would the food."

I buzzed her again. She came in and said, "What?" I cried, "My legs are cold!" She said: "All right, I'll make you a deal. I'll give you a blanket if you promise not to call me in for another ten minutes. I have other patients, you know." I said, "I have very little patience. It's running out fast, too." She said, "Deal?" Knowing it was now or never, I said, "Deal." So she threw the blanket on my legs and left.

I remember the time exactly. It was 9:50. I watched the clock—9:58, 9:59—and buzzed her back in. She came in. By this time she was so mad that I expected to see steam coming out her ears; and she was ready to unplug me, turn the bed around, shove me out of the window, and make it look like an accident. I said, "My legs are cold." She said "Your legs aren't cold," and she left. I knew then that it didn't matter if my legs froze, fell onto the ground, and shattered into a million pieces, she wasn't going to believe that my legs were cold. Finally I just fell asleep.

The next morning I told Mom about this traumatic experience. I pleaded with her, "Mom, you can't leave me tonight." She looked at me with all her motherly wisdom and replied, "Jason, what are the odds that you are going to have the same nurse, same shift, two nights in a row." I thought to myself, "Ah, Mom, you're wiser than I." And the day passed away.

That night, just as my mother left, little Miss Sunshine walked in. She came in and checked my vital signs. I thought, "If I just go to sleep, I'll be O.K." She left and I commenced to fall asleep.

During the night some of the fluid from the pneumonia in my lungs got caught in my tracheal tube and formed a plug, making it impossible for me to breathe. I lay there, unable to breathe, thinking, "Do I die or do I call her in?" Realizing it otherwise meant death, I called her in. "I can't breathe, I can't breathe," I told her. She replied, "Calm down, you can breathe." I thought: Cold legs are one thing; breathing is completely different. "Trust me on this one," I said, "I cannot breathe." Then back and forth: "I can't breathe." "You can breathe." "I can't breathe." "You can breathe." Finally I passed out. And these are the words I heard as I did: "Oh, my ———, he can't breathe." She called a code blue, they brought in the crash cart and hooked me up to the respirator, which I had just barely gotten off. Finally, fifteen minutes later when I was coherent enough to understand, the doctor looked over at me and said, "Jason, if you can't breathe, just tell us." I mean, what's a guy to do?

The following day, in a little talk with the head nurse, I made sure that we wouldn't have another encounter like that.

I worked and worked during therapy, always keeping in sight the end goal of going to rehabilitation. The days passed and the weeks followed. Finally, the glorious day came. The doctors entered my room and proclaimed, "Tomorrow we are going to move you to rehab." Oh man, I was so excited I thought I was going to explode! I could hardly sleep that night. Rehab meant that I was moving up.

The next day I was off to rehabilitation, where I found myself with two new roommates, one on my side of the room and one on the other. What I didn't know was that both of these guys were head trauma cases, that is, someone who has had an accident affecting his mental capacity to think and act. The guy on the other side of the room would lie there and moan all night, "Come on, come on." I thought, "Oh, come on, give the guy what he wants." The guy on my side of the room thought he was in Vietnam. There was a Chinese nurse on the floor, so that didn't work out—he was always trying to kill the nurse and save America. They had him strapped down with two leather straps on each hand and two on each of his legs. The first night I was there he got his mouth to his strap, chewed through both straps on his arms, undid his legs, got out of the bed, got completely naked, and came to my side of the room. I thought to myself, "Well, isn't that special!" I was lying there totally helpless, with one hand protecting my trach to prevent him from trying to start me like a lawn mower and my other hand holding an American flag, "God bless America." I was trying to look as American as possible. The nurse came in, laid him down, and tied him down with something more substantial than straps. Needless to say, I didn't get any sleep that whole week. I would go to bed about one-thirty when I heard the guys both snoring, and I would wake up at about three-thirty so I could be sure to see them wake.

I continued to progress, so they took me out of my traction. They took the tube out of my throat. The day soon came when they said, "Jason, tomorrow you are going to feed yourself breakfast." I was really excited about this! The best thing about it was that I was going to eat the way I wanted to eat. You see, when you are fed in the hospital, once you start your eggs you eat all your eggs; and you eat all your bacon, all your sausage, drink all your juice, eat all your cereal. It's a mother's dream come true. But now I was going to have a little eggs, a little bacon, a little hash browns, a little juice. This wasn't going to be a meal, this was going to be a symphony! So I ordered up, I ordered big—I figured I deserved it.

The next day when they brought my tray it was so full it was bowing in the middle. I started with my Corn Pops. They put on my cuff with a spoon and I prepared to hound down. I got one Corn Pop on the spoon and a little bit of milk, and I was ready. But when I started lifting, I was so weak that it felt like Olympic weight-lifting.

Yet I was lifting for all I was worth. I was telling the Corn Pop, Go to the mouth, go to the mouth, but it fell. There I was, huffing and puffing, totally drained. I went for another, and it fell too. (Guys, you can sympathize with me. This kind of thing puts a serious dent in your masculinity. A fine-looking lady comes up to you and says, "What do you lift?" "Well," you reply, "I do one Corn Pop, three reps, four rounds.") Finally, six Corn Pops later, I got one. I skipped therapy that day and—I kid you not—took a four-hour nap—all over one stinking Corn Pop.

It was then that I realized I had very little physical control of my life. What I did have, what I had never lost, was *mental* control of my life. What is mental control of our lives? I believe it is attitude, and I have broken the word *attitude* down into what I think are its components:

A for A
T for Totally
T for Terrific
I for Idea
T for To
U for Undermine
D for Decreased
E for Esteem

A Totally Terrific Idea To Undermine Decreased Esteem.

What is esteem? Esteem is a high regard, and I think we have two types of esteem. Number one, self-esteem, and number two, life esteem. First, self-esteem.

One of the big contributing factors for our self-esteem is our friends. A friend of mine from the Portland Trailblazers, Danny Ainge, wrote me this in a letter: "I like to be around winners. It is a lot easier to succeed in life when you surround yourself with people who give 100 percent, never quit, and are willing to pay the price." How true that is! It is so much easier to attain our highest goals of seminary graduation, missions, and temple marriage, and ultimately life in the celestial kingdom, if our friends share those same goals. If we will just be careful whom we choose to associate with, friends can be great contributors to our positive self-image. So be with people who feel good about themselves. With people who have strong gospel testimonies. With people who know where they are going, and who know where they have been. These are the kinds of friends we should want to have in the Church. And we should make friends with good people too who are not in the Church, and seek to introduce them to the gospel.

The second thing is that we need to realize our countless blessings. At home I have a list that I call "I Can or I Am." It's a hundred things that I can do or that I am. Number one is the fact that I am a member of this Church. Number two is that I can see, and number three is that I can hear. Number four and five are that I can touch and I can taste. The list continues to name some of my numerous blessings. It is so easy to think of ourselves as lacking blessings, but I believe that as we come to recognize some of the blessings we do have but which we take for granted, we can feel our Heavenly Father's love more directly and in turn can have a more positive self-image. Actually we are blessed sometimes in ways that seem too small to notice. You will realize this as you compile your own list: the first things you list will be big and easily noticeable, things like health, strength, and family, things we hear of often in the prayer at the dinner table. But as you reach the end of your list you will begin to list things that are much smaller yet are blessings just the same.

When we focus on our blessings our trials don't seem so dim. In the hospital, whenever I felt down I would sit in front of a mirror and move my wrist up and down, up and down, up and down. You see, the break Rich (the guy in the other room) had was one pin head higher than mine, and because of that he could not do that with his wrists. I used to think to myself, Look at how lucky you are, Jason. What a blessing this is in your life. Look at all the things you can do because you can move your wrists. And I'd do it for hours sometimes, switching hands. The more I did it, the more blessed I felt and the better I felt about myself, the more I realized that I didn't have it all that hard, that many people had it a lot harder than I had. And as I did this I felt rejuvenated, lucky to be alive, and I would be positive once again.

Here, then, is a challenge for you. Whenever you feel down, stand in front of a mirror and think to yourself, Look at how blessed I am because I have the muscles and I have the faculties that let me stand up, and I can run, I can play, I can dance. Look at your blessings in that light. Do you recognize these blessings and use them for good? Do you take your talents and blessings and bury them, or do you use them in positive, good ways?

Self-esteem can also grow as a person lives a life that makes him proud to be who he is. I'll illustrate this with a story about my little brother, Nathan, who is now a fourth grader. A few years ago, his school teacher sent home with him an activity he had done. Once when I was by the refrigerator, where we always stick Nathan's activities, I saw this and thought I'd read it. The first question was, "What do you want to be in ten years?" He had written, "A pro football player." I thought, What ambition! The next question was, "What do you want to be in a week?" He wrote, "A kid." I thought, What a comedian! The last question was, "What do you want to be today?" He responded, "Nathan." I thought, What wisdom! He was confident of himself, and his life was such that he was proud to be who he was that day. If I passed out that same questionnaire now, I wonder how many of you would be able to answer that last question with your name. I pray that I might live my life so as never to be ashamed to be me. Especially on that great and dreadful day when I must report to the judgment bar, I hope I will be glad to be Jason Hall.

The second thing is life esteem. Life esteem is the way we look at life. William James said that we can alter our lives by simply altering our attitudes. How true! If we don't like something in our lives, in many cases all we need to do is change our mindset. Then as we change our ways we will change the thing we don't like. It might take a lot of work. Sometimes it might take some repentance. Sometimes it might take going to the bishop. But in such cases we *can* change the thing we don't like in our lives. Many people want to change but simply sit around doing nothing and wishing they were different. Of this President Thomas S. Monson has said, "Work will win where wishy-washy wishing won't."

Another great determinant in our life esteem is whether we look for the glass to be "half empty or half full." Do we look for the good in life? It is much easier to find, dwell on, and accent the negative, but our challenge is to search out the positive. Not only that, but we must try to find and bring out the best in all we meet. There is just as much water as air in the glass, so the question is whether we see the empty or the full.

Finally one of my favorite quotations: "It's not what life does with you; It's what you do with life." One thing I can promise: each of us will experience adversity until the day we die. There will be things we don't like about ourselves and about our life. The challenge is to take those problems and master them, for the difference between a stepping stone and a stumbling block is six inches between the ears.

In life we will have some extreme highs and tremendous lows, and our job is to make the best of both. We must never quit, for the challenge lies in going on. We must work hard, do our best.

I love my family. I love my friends. And most important, I love my Heavenly Father, I know he loves me and I know he loves you. The gospel of Jesus Christ is true; I know this as surely as I know anything, for I have tested it in my own life and I know that it works. That we might one day all have a reunion in a place far greater than this is my humble prayer.

Stephen Jason Hall, a student at Brigham Young University, grew up in Idaho. He enjoys music, public speaking, plays, basketball, and BYU football. An Eagle Scout, while in high school Jason was junior class president, community education coach, and member of the seminary council. At BYU he is an executive director in student government and is on the Honor Code Committee.

12

The Dating Years: Charting a Safe Course

Randal A. Wright

When I was about thirteen years old our family took a vacation in the West, on which the highlight of the trip was touring Carlsbad Caverns in New Mexico. My cousin and I couldn't wait to enter the cave. Seeing our eagerness to explore *all* the 640 acres open to visitors, my father decided to stay above while we went the 829 feet down to the floor of the caverns.

Our guide gave us interesting details of the interior of the cave. Since he had the only light, we stayed real close to him at first. He pointed out dangers along the trail and the bats inhabiting the cave, repeatedly warning us to stay on the marked paths. As the tour progressed, my cousin and I paid little attention to these warnings and began to lag behind the main group.

At one point of interest the guide invited the group to gather in close to him. We two were off down the trail and didn't hear him. He said he would turn the lights off to let us see how dark the caverns are. When he flipped the switch, we found ourselves enveloped in a darkness like no other. It frightened me badly, especially knowing we were away from the safety of our guide. I was never more relieved than when he switched the light back on. We stayed much closer to the guide for the rest of the tour. When our journey through the cavern was over I was very happy to see my father again as we came to the surface.

One of the most successful tools Satan uses in our day to keep us from accomplishing our earthly missions is immorality. He throws many temptations in our way and would enjoy seeing us stumble and fall. His is a life of darkness and misery (as in the cave), and he desires company.

But our loving Heavenly Father has offered us a special guide who has safety rules for us to follow so we can have successful dating experiences during our teenage years. These guidelines have been repeatedly stated by our latter-day prophets and are available for us to read and follow. They provide the help we need to withstand Satan's temptings. By following the prophet, we are not left in the dark. These inspired rules from our prophets mark a bright path to true happiness and can lead to a temple marriage, with fun in dating and socializing along the way.

Some of you may ask, "What does a ninety-two-year-old man know about the teenage dating scene of today, since he hasn't dated in over seventy years?" Well, that question is a lot like asking a master mechanic with seventy years experience what he knows about changing the spark plugs in a car. During their years in the Lord's service our prophets have dealt with thousands of cases of immorality. But our prophet has far greater insight than experience only. He receives direct inspiration and revelation from the Lord. The Lord and his prophet want us to be truly happy. With that in mind, let's look at a few guidelines that, if followed, will help you chart a safe course through the dating years.

Keep good company. "Be careful in the selection of your friends. If in the presence of certain persons you are lifted to nobler heights, you are in good company. But if your friends or associates encourage base thoughts, then you had best leave them." (Ezra Taft Benson, *God, Family, Country* [Salt Lake City: Deseret Book Company, 1974], p. 241.)

The word *company* does not mean only your friends or associates. Television, movies, music, and books we read can also be friend or foe. The places we choose to enter can influence us for good or bad. We must stay on the marked path; the one that will make us feel happy forever, not gratified for just a moment.

No dating until age sixteen, and then only double or group dating. For many years the Church has tried diligently to discourage youth from early dating and also from single dating until the proper time. "Group social activities should be provided as alternatives to early dating or to activities that encourage teenagers to pair off. . . . Some youth who do pair off exclusively in their early teens are emotionally and socially immature. That is one reason why the Church counsels youth to date only after age 16, and even then not to pair off exclusively with one partner." (*Young Women Handbook*, 1988, p.

20.) Here again, when we place ourselves in situations that we have been counseled against we risk disaster.

Many are confused about what a *date* actually is. I have discussed this subject many times with my seminary and institute students. They had different answers and opinions, but finally we came up with a definition that everyone agreed with. A date means a pairing off with one person for the duration of an activity. A date does not necessarily mean the formal process of a boy calling a girl, asking her to go somewhere for a specific time, then driving to her home to pick her up. There are formal dates as well as informal or casual dates. Here are some case studies. You decide (honestly) whether each would be defined as a date or not:

1. A fourteen-year-old young woman invites a fifteen-year-old young man to a stake dance. They are together all evening, not dancing with anyone else. Is this a date?

President Spencer W. Kimball had this to say about dances: "For a youth to dance all evening with one partner, which we might call 'monopolistic' dancing, is not only antisocial but it circumscribes one's legitimate pleasures and opportunities. Also it can encourage improper intimacies by its exclusiveness." (*The Miracle of Forgiveness* [Salt Lake City: Bookcraft, 1969], p. 222.)

2. A thirteen-year-old boy asks a girl of the same age to meet him at a high school homecoming game. Since he cannot drive, his parents take him. He buys the girl a corsage; she buys him a boutonniere. They are together for the duration of the game and are seen holding hands. Both say this is not a date. What do you say?

A young woman in one of my institute classes said, "I think what the prophet is telling us is that we shouldn't be pairing off with anyone before the proper time." Some may still question why the prophet has counseled our teens not to date until age sixteen when all their school friends are allowed to. I have found no better evidence to back this counsel than that provided by two Utah researchers. The findings from their five-year study on teen pregnancy are unmistakable. They polled 2,200 teenagers in New Mexico, Utah, Arizona, and California. Of the girls who had begun dating at age twelve, 91 percent had sexual relations before graduating from high school. Of the girls who started dating at age thirteen, the number was 56 percent. Of those who began dating at age fourteen the number was 53 percent, and of those who began dating at age fifteen the number was 40 percent. But of the young women who waited until sixteen to begin dating, only 20 percent were sexually active before high school graduation. (*Church News,* September 10, 1988, p. 16.)

Pairing off at such a young age presents a very real moral danger for the future. "The recreational and social activities of the crowd can be wholesome and entertaining. Physical and moral safety is increased in the multiplicity of friends." (Spencer W. Kimball, *The Miracle of Forgiveness*, p. 221.)

Don't place yourself in the position where the chance of being immoral is greatly increased. Double or group dating after age sixteen, with a variety of different people, increases one's safety and is also much more fun!

Date only worthy members of the Church. Remember the importance of proper dating. President Kimball gave some wise counsel on this subject: "Clearly, right marriage begins with right dating. . . . Therefore, this warning comes with great emphasis. Do not take the chance of dating nonmembers, or members who are untrained and faithless. [You] may say, 'Oh, I do not intend to marry this person. It is just a "fun" date.' But one cannot afford to take a chance on falling in love with someone who may never accept the gospel." (*The Miracle of Forgiveness*, pp. 241–42.)

"Our Heavenly Father wants you to date young women who are faithful members of the Church, who encourage you to serve a full-time mission and to magnify your priesthood" (Ezra Taft Benson, *Ensign*, May 1966, p. 45).

I have heard several questions and comments about this counsel. Why would the prophet come out so strongly about this subject in general conference? First of all, let's remember that this is not just the prophet's counsel. He appears to be relaying a message to us. His statement reads, "Our Heavenly Father wants you to date young women who are faithful members of the Church." So, actually, the question should be, Why does Heavenly Father feel this to be so important?

What is wrong with dating nonmembers as long as it's just for fun? Very few marriages occur without the couple first having a fun date. The old saying "You marry who you date" is literally true in our society.

What if you live in an area where there are few worthy members to date? This can be a real challenge. Make sure you attend all your Young Men and Young Women activities, youth conferences, and other stake events. They will provide opportunities to meet youth from other areas.

What about missionary work? Presidents Benson and Kimball are two of the greatest missionaries of our time. They definitely would not discourage missionary work, but would instead endorse the right way to do it. We can still have group activities that nonmembers are invited to, without pairing off. It is possible to have fun with our nonmember friends and do missionary work while following the prophet's counsel.

No going steady during the teen years. "A vicious, destructive, social pattern of early steady dating must be changed," wrote Elder Spencer W. Kimball. "It is my considered feeling, having had some experience in interviewing youth, that the change of this one pattern of social activities of our youth would immediately eliminate a majority of the sins of our young folks." ("Save the Youth of Zion," *Improvement Era,* September 1965, p. 806.)

Why would not going steady help keep a youth on a safe course through the dating years? Going steady seems to promise a secure relationship, a date every weekend, someone to care about. At least, that's the way it sometimes seems to young people. But here are some reasons for *not* going steady.

1. Going steady prior to a mission can interfere with a young man's decision to serve and with a missionary's effectiveness once he is serving. President Ezra Taft Benson advised: "Avoid steady dating with a young man prior to the time of his mission call. If your relationship with him is more casual, then he can make that decision to serve more easily and also can concentrate his full energies on his missionary work instead of the girlfriend back home." (Pres. Benson, "To the Young Women of the Church," *Ensign,* November 1986, pp. 82–83.)

2. Their friendships are lessened when young people go steady. They usually limit the opportunity of meeting new people and developing new friendships. To develop our personalities we all need interaction with many people in social settings. Going steady limits this interaction, without which a person lacks the social exposure to make a wise decision on a marriage partner when the time comes.

3. Jealousy and insecurity increase. Young couples become tied down and restricted. One girl commented, "Instead of going steady, I wound up staying home steady because of his jealousy." Oftentimes teens are too young to handle the strong emotions they feel with a steady partner. Many constantly worry about who that partner is talking to or where he or she is going.

Most become extremely possessive of the partner. Courting during the teen years is filled with doubts and apprehensions. Why is she looking at him? Is she prettier than I am? Will we marry? With the maturity arrived at when the proper time for courting comes (after missions for young men), doubts leave and certainty replaces jealousy. Most steadies become very preoccupied. They think of their steady almost constantly during their waking hours. Schoolwork, seminary, scripture study, and even household chores often suffer. It often becomes difficult for some teens to even carry on a conversation without the boyfriend's or girlfriend's name coming up. At a time when youth should be thinking about schoolwork, talent development, homemaking skills, and mission preparation, many are spending almost every waking hour thinking about love and marriage. It is not courtship but friendship that should be the relationship between teenagers.

4. Immorality and early marriages increase. One family researcher has defined going steady as "acting like you are already married while still living at your parents' home." Going steady tends to give the young man a sense of familiarity or ownership, and to the young girl a feeling of belonging to someone—just as in marriage! This greatly increases the chances of their becoming immoral.

The rising incidence of teen pregnancy is frightening. How many of these young girls were going steady at the time they became pregnant? The number one reason for early marriage, according to research, is pregnancy. The number two reason is early dating.

5. Family life becomes disrupted when a teen goes steady. Too often the boy is either over at the girl's house or on the phone with her—or they are out together. A teenager who is going steady often does not want to do much with the family.

Oftentimes youth, and even their parents, deny they are going steady when it is obvious that they are. If a ring or other token of promise is not involved, then they are just "good friends," even if they date only each other and even talk about when they marry. If a boy and girl are exclusively paired off, a ring does not need to be involved—they are going steady.

President Spencer W. Kimball has said, "Young men and women, not yet ready for marriage, should be friends with many others, but they should not engage in courting" (Edward L. Kimball, ed., *The Teachings of Spencer W. Kimball* [Salt Lake City: Bookcraft, 1982], p. 288). The benefits of not going steady during the teen years are great.

Do not kiss improperly. "Kissing has been prostituted and has degenerated to develop and express lust instead of affection, honor, and admiration. To kiss in casual dating is asking for trouble. What do kisses mean when given out like pretzels and robbed of sacredness? What is miscalled the 'soul kiss' is an abomination and stirs passions to the eventual loss of virtue. Even if timely courtship justifies the kiss, it should be a clean, decent, sexless one like the kiss between mother and son, or father and daughter." (*The Teachings of Spencer W. Kimball,* p. 281.)

Kissing should mean something special. Usually when a young man kisses a girl he gives the message that he likes her a lot. Unfortunately some boys are only playing games with the girl, and feelings can be hurt as a result.

Several years ago I heard about a young man who claimed to hold the record in his stake for kissing the most girls in one day. According to reports, he had kissed six different girls that day and was very proud of this feat. This seemed unusual to me, so I looked forward to a casual conversation with him to discuss his dating practices.

One day the opportunity came. After we had visited for a while, the subject of dating and finally kissing came up. I asked about his ideas on kissing. He let me know that he thought he should kiss as many girls as possible before his mission, to see if he was compatible with any. I asked him how many girls he had kissed. His response: "So many that I can't keep count! In fact, I really don't believe if they all walked through the door right now I would even recognize them all." I was surprised, but smiled so he'd keep talking. I finally asked, "How many in one day?" "Six," came the quick reply. "And that was all before 2:00 P.M. I stayed with the same girl after that for the rest of the day." He told me that he was at a high school event when this took place. I asked if the girls were LDS. He slowly shook his head, but quickly added that it wasn't a date.

I asked him if he had ever heard what President Kimball had taught on the subject of kissing. He sheepishly said no.

"Do you want to hear it?" I asked.

"Not really, but go ahead."

I then read him the above statement. His comment was, "Well, I have given out so many pretzels, there is no need to stop now!" We continued to talk, and I asked him if he had anyone in mind to date when he got home from his mission. His answer surprised me. One of the top young women on his list was one that we both knew had set a goal to kiss no one until she was sure they would marry.

The next day when I saw the young man again, I said: "Guess what! Your kissing record has been beaten!"

"No way! I know no one around here has beaten it," came his startled reply.

"Yes, it happened!"

"Who?"

"Your future wife!" I calmly replied. "She had the same goal as you, and kissed seven different nonmember guys in one day."

He looked shocked and said, "But you don't know who my future wife is."

"You're right," I said, "but I'm telling you who you deserve!"

"I guess I do have a double standard, don't I?" he said. "I have never thought of it in that way before."

Immorality does not usually begin with necking or petting. It begins with kissing. Then come sexual thoughts. These grow whenever entertained, until the strong become weak and yield to temptation. To help you prepare for a temple marriage, imagine your future wife or husband doing the identical things you do. This will help you avoid temptations, and then you'll be prepared when the time is right for finding an eternal companion.

Be courteous to your parents. President David O. McKay said: "Parents who do not know where their children are at night are recreant [disloyal] to the sacred obligation of parenthood and untrue to the high ideals of the Church regarding home life" (Conference Report, October 1951, p. 10).

As a safeguard and also a courtesy, let your parents know where you are going, who you'll be with, and when they can expect you home. Upon your arrival home, sit down with your parents to discuss the evening's activities. This provides great safety. You surely would not feel comfortable discussing your evening if you had done something wrong. I have a friend who told me that his after-date discussions with his mom kept him on the marked path. He had been tempted many times to be immoral, but knowing that he would be talking to his mom about the evening's activities and giving her a goodnight kiss kept him clean.

Obedience to our prophet's counsel brings safety and happiness. Our path *is* brightly marked; now we must chart the course we will follow. What will yours be?

Randal A. Wright, an institute director in Beaumont, Texas, and former editor of a sports magazine, lists his interests and likes as speaking to the youth, waterparks, basketball, autobiographies, and country/Western music. He says the youth of today are "the royal generation saved to prepare the way for the Savior's return." Randal and his wife, Wendy, have five children.

13

Yagottawanna Win

Suzanne L. Hansen

Have you ever looked in the mirror and said to yourself, "How on earth (or in heaven, for that matter) could anyone ever love that face?"

It's not surprising if you feel that way. In this hyped-up world full of glamorous, cover-girl faces, totally trim bodies, or bulging biceps, many of us see ourselves on the losing end.

The real losers, however, are made so by loser attitudes, not by looks. The real losers throw too many "personal pity-parties," where "poor me" is the only guest. All they talk about is what is going wrong—their hang-ups, their negative qualities, and what they don't have, wish they had, and aren't blessed with. They concentrate on their flaws.

"If only . . ." becomes the losers' cry. "If only I had better looks. If only I was smarter. If only I had money, a car, and a date, this world would be great!"

Stop! Think!

Our Father in Heaven creates only winners!

Each day winners celebrate life and all the things *they can do.* The face they see in the mirror is that of a child of God who has unlimited potential.

You see, we all have powers to make things happen. So stop waiting for someone to make your day. Make your own day.

"W" Mitchell of Genessee Park, Colorado, is living proof that the right kind of winning attitude can turn you into a winner. He has a lot of strikes against him. Mitchell's face is a patchwork of

multicolored skin grafts. The fingers of both hands are either miss-
ing or mere stubs. And his paralyzed legs lie thin and useless.

No one is bold enough to ask what happened. Some guess he
was injured in a car wreck. The real story is more astounding than
anyone could guess. Mitchell, as he likes to be called in honor of his
stepfather, was horrifically burned and nearly killed in a freak
motorcycle accident. Then his back was broken in a plane crash,
leaving him paralyzed from the waist down.

Before the accidents he had so many dreams and plans—so
many things he wanted to do.

He remembers well his beautiful new motorcycle that he rode
to work. In an instant a laundry truck collided with him. As he
went down he crushed his elbow and fractured his pelvis. At the
same time the gas cap of his motorcycle popped off and he was
drenched with gasoline. All at once the heat from his smashed
motorcycle's engine ignited the gasoline, covering him with flames
and burning over sixty-five percent of his body.

A quick-witted fellow in a nearby car saved Mitchell's life by
dousing him with a fire extinguisher. But his face had been burned
off, his fingers were black and twisted, and his legs were nothing
but raw, red flesh.

Mitchell lay unconscious for two weeks while a round-the-
clock team of doctors battled to keep him alive. It was not uncom-
mon for some first-time visitors to look at him and faint.

Four months after the accident, he had received thirteen blood
transfusions, sixteen skin graft operations, and other surgeries. But
all this time he was in remarkably high spirits. In fact, right after he
became conscious he asked for his flying books so he could start
studying for his pilot's license. One of his dreams was to be a pilot.

"He had a spirit like I've never seen before or since," says Dr.
Mark Gorney, Mitchell's plastic surgeon.

Mitchell says the secret of his happy attitude is twofold. First,
the love, faith, and encouragement of friends and family. Second,
his personal philosophy. He realized he did not have to buy society's notion that one must be handsome or good looking in order
to be healthy and happy.

"I'm in charge of my own space ship," Mitchell says. "It's my
ups, my downs. I can choose to see this situation as a setback or as a
starting point."

Once out of the hospital, he says, he spent "a lot of time trying
to figure out how to do stuff." Even a stiff breeze brought agony. "I
could not pick up a fork, take my pants off, go to the bathroom
without help, or dial a phone."

But he determinedly set to work learning to do all those things again. Six months after the accident he was flying a plane, and eventually he received his pilot's license.

Early one morning he and four friends took off in a small plane. The plane lurched off the runway and flew oddly, lost power, and dropped like a rock back onto the runway.

Excruciating pain shot up from Mitchell's lower back as the plane hit the concrete. "I told the others to get out," he recalls, "but I couldn't move my legs." His lower back was broken and his spinal cord damaged beyond repair. He was now a paraplegic. His life became a living nightmare.

As you can imagine, Mitchell had his dark moments, and he sometimes wondered what he'd done to deserve all these problems and pain. But he still had his faith, his family, and his friends, and that profound sense that he could create his own destiny by focusing on the "cans" rather than on the "can'ts."

He recalls that one day he met a nineteen-year-old in the hospital's gymnasium. Like Mitchell, this young man had been paralyzed. He had been a mountain climber and a super-active, outdoor person. Now he was convinced that his life was totally over.

Mitchell remembers: "I went over to this kid and said, 'You know something? Before all of this happened to me there were ten thousand things I could do. Now there are nine thousand. I could spend the rest of my life dwelling on the one thousand that I lost. But I choose to focus on the nine thousand that are left.' "

Mitchell started to follow the advice of the German philosopher Goethe: "Whatever you can do, or dream you can, begin it. Boldness has genius, power, and magic in it."

Since his two accidents, Mitchell has become a successful businessman, a respected environmentalist, a sought-after speaker, and mayor of his town. He also has run for Congress. He even rafts down rivers and is a sky-diver. And he has become a happy husband.

Mitchell met his future wife, Annie, when she was a nurse's aide at the hospital where he was undergoing therapy after his paralysis. She recalls meeting him: "He has such a great sense of humor and puts you so at ease that after ten minutes you forget that he looks different at all."

For four years Mitchell wooed Annie, but she resisted. He called her one day and asked her out to dinner. She said, "You sure are persistent," and she refused again. She could tell by the disappointed tone in his voice that he had been hurt and probably would not call her again.

It was then she realized that she wanted to get to know him better. She called him back.

Since they've been married, Annie says, "It's gotten better every year. We not only love one another, but we really like each other, too."

"My life," Mitchell says, "proves that all limitations are very self-imposed. It's not what happens to you in life, it's what you do about it that really counts."

Yagottawanna. And if you do—well, a loving Heavenly Father has given you everything you need to succeed. Problems really can be opportunities in disguise.

Chances are your fingers and face have not been burned off. And probably you can walk and run anywhere you want. It's your attitude that's either helping or hurting you.

I have a dear friend who has an "I can" attitude. Her outlook on life has inspired me and many others. She has what a lot of people would call problems. But she doesn't see it that way.

Her name is Kathy Vorwaller. She was born with a malformed body. She has no arms at all, and has one leg that is very short and has no knee joint. The other leg is normal, but the foot has only four toes.

Kathy admits that her disability was a mystery. But she really doesn't dwell on it. She says in her matter-of-fact way, "This is just one of those things that happens in life."

The Vorwaller parents treated Kathy as normal to whatever extent was possible, with responsibilities and opportunities like those of their other children. Kathy's mother, Inga, always reminded her that God doesn't make mistakes, that Kathy was born with everything she needed to be successful in life.

Kathy doesn't like to bump her head when she falls, so on the way down she tries to catch herself with her shoulder. This process has resulted in a snapped collar bone seven times. She has also had two broken legs.

But Kathy has made things happen in her life. With an artificial leg attached to her short leg, she conquered public schools, graduating from high school. Determined to enjoy normal activities, she has learned to use her feet as hands. She does needlepoint, types, programs computers, plays chess, and even puts on her own makeup with her toes. And with great zeal and enthusiasm she also rides horseback, camps with her family, water skis, roller skates, and dreams of sky diving.

How many of us with all our limbs enjoy and use them so fully for fun and growth? But, yagottawanna!

At the Utah State Fair Kathy has even won the top honor for her stitchery. She graduated from Salt Lake Community College, and today she works for Utah Transit Authority as a computer programmer.

When I asked Kathy how she does it all, she smiled and said, "I just get down on my one knee and thank God every day for my foot that works."

If you want things to be different, you must be different. First, change your attitude. If you want a brighter, happier life, be a brighter, happier person. It all starts with how you think.

Your mind is the most powerful computer in the universe. You have eighteen billion brain cells all trembling with excitement to go to work on something, to help you become a real winner. Yet scientists tell us that we use only about ten percent of our mental capacity. If that's true, the only person holding you back in life is yourself.

If you really "wanna" take charge of your life, here are seven steps to that goal:

1. *Love God.* Recognize each day the person who has given you everything you need to become a winner—your Heavenly Father. Express love and gratitude to him each day. Count your blessings and your gains, not your losses. As you do these things your heart will expand and your mind will soar.

2. *Love yourself.* Every day, list on paper those things you did that made you feel happy and successful that day. If you're having a hard time filling a page, don't worry. Start by finding *one* thing a day that you can write down. Soon it will become a flood when you realize that you are a good person and can do good things. You're a winner. Tell yourself that in the mirror each day.

3. *Love your neighbor.* Remember the way to get love is to give it. Life gives to the giver and takes from the taker. If you ever feel a lack of love—if you ever feel that you're not getting enough love—give yourself away. As often as possible, say to people, "Here, let me help you." Then watch the love come back to you.

4. *Be a love radiator.* Here's what to do:
   a. Smile a lot to others.
   b. Send lots of love notes and thank-you notes.
   c. Be responsive to and interested in others.
   d. Be cheerful. Remember, no one likes a frowny face!
   e. Give out a lot of sincere compliments. It's fun when you shock people by telling them that they look nice or you like what they did. It will make you feel good, too.

5. *Dare to hug.* If you put your arm around someone, it's a way of saying, "I think you are a fine person." The famous phone commercial says, "Reach out and touch someone." Literally show your approval by giving a sincere hug to someone who needs it.

6. *Work toward goals.* Just as Mitchell, after the terrible plane crash that left him paralyzed for the rest of his life, had a goal to fly again and to sky dive, you too can move boldly toward attaining your dreams.

Kathy had a goal to learn how to write with her toes. Not only has she accomplished that, but she types, programs computers, cross stitches, and can do hundreds of things with her very flexible toes.

Goals are like magnets. They pull us toward good things. They are commitments you make to yourself. When you write them down, it's easier to commit your whole mind to your goals.

7. *Never give up or give in.* Thomas Edison is one of the best examples of this principle. He wasn't always respected in his day as he is today. Once an interviewer asked him, "Mr. Edison, what have you got to say about the fact that you've failed thousands of times in your attempts to create a light bulb?" Edison replied: "I beg your pardon, but I've never failed even once. I've had *thousands of learning experiments* that didn't work. I had to run through enough learning experiences to find a way that it *did* work."

You see, properly speaking there is no such thing as a failure or a loser. We just haven't had enough learning experiences yet. The Lord has said we are to endure to the end and he must have a reason for that counsel. I believe life is like a race — but you are only running against yourself. The winners are the ones who won't give in or give up.

As Alicia Fuller wrote to her high school 1990 track team:

No one can ever make you want to be the best.
It's all up to you.
Yagottawanna if you're ever gonna.
Yagottawanna bad enough to try.
Yagottawanna bad enough to win.

I believe in you. God believes in you. You can be a winner in all you do and make an incredible difference. But before it will happen, yagottawanna.

*Suzanne L. Hansen, author of five books and a lec-
turer and businesswoman in Salt Lake City, was
college homecoming queen and in 1980 and 1981
was named one of the Outstanding Young Women
in America. Arts and crafts, flower arranging,
classical music, and new age music are included in
her list of favorite things. Suzanne and her husband, Michael, have three children.*

14

Integrity:
What's Your Price?

Vivian R. Cline

Integrity, the final value of the Young Women theme, is something that seems rare in today's world. Psychologists refer to integrity as situational. In other words, it's all right to have integrity if it's to your advantage; but if it's not to your advantage, don't trouble yourself.

LDS young women recognize these words: "I will have the moral courage to make my actions consistent with my knowledge of right and wrong." But do we do as the words suggest?

One of my favorite examples of integrity is that of Joseph who was sold into Egypt. As you will recall, Jacob loved Joseph more than his other children (see Genesis 37:3), which the historian Josephus attributes to "the virtues of [Joseph's] mind, for he excelled the rest in prudence" (*Antiquities of the Jews*, II, II, 1). Thus Jacob showed Joseph favor.

In that day and time, colors in cloth were hard to come by. Dyes were derived from various plants and vegetables and usually had to be imported. Most fabrics were just left in their natural state of beige, tan, or brown. From Jacob, however, Joseph was fortunate enough to get not only a colored coat but one of many colors.

How do you suppose that made his older brothers feel? A little jealous maybe? Are you kidding? They were chapped! In fact, they were so upset that some even wanted to kill Joseph. Reuben, however, prevented this, and while he was absent Judah later stepped in and recommended that instead they sell their young brother as a slave. The others agreed, and they quickly sold him to a group of Ishmeelite merchants going to Egypt. At that point they took his coat, made tears in it, and dipped it in animal blood. This would allow them to convince their father that Joseph had been devoured by wild beasts.

When the Ishmeelites arrived in Egypt they sold Joseph to a man named Potiphar, the captain of the guard in Pharaoh's army and a man of means. He had servants and material possessions. Potiphar noticed, however, that when Joseph came to be his servant, everything Joseph handled prospered. He knew that the Lord was with Joseph, so he put Joseph in charge of everything he owned—except his wife.

The scripture says, "His master's wife cast her eyes upon Joseph; and she said, Lie with me" (Genesis 39:7). Tell me, is this the direct approach or what? No beating around the bush for her.

Josephus tells us that she had "fallen in love with [Joseph], both on account of his beauty of body and his dexterous management of affairs" (*Antiquities*, II, IV, 2). There was, I believe, an even greater attraction that Potiphar's wife felt for Joseph that no historian ever mentions. You see, there is a special glow that men possess when they are morally pure and clean—an inner strength of confidence and self-assuredness that women can feel. I think Potiphar's wife recognized that glow.

Joseph tried in a kind way to explain to her why he couldn't respond to her advances. He told her he couldn't betray his master's trust in him, nor could he commit that great sin against God. This refusal only spurred her interest, and she continued to make advances.

A further scriptural comment is significant to our understanding the temptations of Satan. It says, "And it came to pass, as she spake to Joseph day by day, that he hearkened not unto her, to lie by her, or to be with her" (Genesis 39:10).

We are not just occasionally tempted by peers to do something wrong. We are tempted day by day, over and over. It's extremely important that we stay strong and close to the Lord so we will have the strength to persevere. And that is what Joseph did.

One day Joseph went into the house to take care of some business. I feel sure he was unaware that there were no other men in the house, or he would not have entered. Potiphar's wife knew there were no men there, however, and she waited to make her final move.

As he entered, she grabbed his coat or outer garment and said, "Lie with me." Joseph knew that talking about it would do no good; he had tried that before. The scriptures tell us simply that he "got him out." Joseph left so quickly that his coat remained behind in the clutches of this designing woman.

Again, and for the last time, Potiphar's wife had been refused. She was so upset that she decided she would make Joseph pay for her pain. She immediately summoned the "men of the house" (presumably from the grounds) and told them that Joseph had tried to take advantage of her. As proof, she even had the coat he had left behind. When her husband returned home she related the same false story to him; and, believing her, he was angry at Joseph.

Potiphar immediately had Joseph cast into prison. Now, was that fair? Did Joseph do anything wrong? No. All he did was make his actions consistent with his knowledge of right and wrong. Where did it get him? In prison.

While in prison, Joseph interpreted the dreams of Pharaoh's chief baker and his chief butler, who had been placed there after falling into disfavor with their master. The interpretations were correct, so when the Pharaoh had a dream that the wise men of his court could not interpret, his chief butler, now released from prison, said, "I know of someone who will be able to help." Pharaoh sent for Joseph; Joseph interpreted Pharaoh's dream; the interpretation was correct; and Pharaoh promoted Joseph to be second in command in all Egypt. (See Genesis 37, 39–41.)

Joseph was a man of integrity. In exercising it he first had to pay a price, but ultimately he was greatly blessed for it. This is a normal pattern: first, we claim to have integrity; second, that integrity is questioned or tested; third, we experience pain or opposition. But when we determine to hold true thereafter, we experience great rewards.

When my husband and I were first married we were both in college full-time and working part-time and I was pregnant with our first child. Money therefore was extremely tight. I remember having only forty dollars a month to spend on groceries. I learned very quickly that a way to stretch my food budget was to use coupons. Clipping coupons and using them when the items were on sale helped me get more for my money.

Because our income was so small those first couple of years, we began an enjoyable Christmas tradition. Instead of purchasing expensive presents for each other, we would go to a nice grocery store and buy Christmas groceries together. Doug would take a grocery cart and I would take a second one and we would go down the aisles of the store selecting items we normally couldn't afford to buy. It was so much fun buying ham, turkey, olives, mushrooms, pop, and all those other delicious things that were usually out of our range.

When we went on this Christmas shopping spree one year, I did not take a shopping list, because I knew I would be impulse shopping. The problem with this was that I didn't know which coupons to take; so I took them all.

After loading our carts up with all our delicacies, we went to the checkout stand.

At this particular store it was customary to give the cashier the coupons first, before you paid. I looked at the two huge carts bulging with food and then at my stack of coupons. I had no idea what coupon items we were purchasing. Hesitantly I took a small stack of the coupons and placed them on the counter. After all, I knew I had purchased those items at one time or another . . . in my life.

The cashier looked me straight in the face and said, "Do you have products for each of these coupons?"

Pausing, and with a deep swallow, I said, "Yes."

The cashier picked up the top coupon as she said, "Let's see, Charmin bathroom tissue." Quickly looking through my cart, she said, "I don't seem to see any Charmin." I swallowed hard again as she picked up the second coupon and said: "Delmonte catsup. I don't seem to see any Delmonte, either."

If I could have shrunk down to the size of a munchkin and slipped out of that store, I would have. I felt so embarrassed. I could not believe what I had just done. For the price of a couple of dollars' worth of stupid coupons I had lost my integrity. Then and there I vowed that never again—never under any circumstances nor for any price—would I allow my integrity to be questioned.

A few years later I had the chance to prove myself. The year was 1980. It was a very difficult year for me. My husband had changed careers and in doing so had taken a 50 percent cut in salary. In order to make ends meet, suddenly I found it necessary to work full-time managing a women's health spa. I don't like working full-time. I love being a wife and mother, but at that point in time I had no other choice.

This was a difficult year for many Church members. It was the year that the Equal Rights Amendment had been proposed to Congress. This proposed amendment to the United States Constitution, intended to lead to exactly equal rights for men and women, was a highly controversial initiative that many saw as being bound to result in great disservice to women. Though the Church never takes a stand on political issues, it does take stands on moral issues, and in this case the Brethren saw moral implications and recommended that we not support the amendment in its poorly written and easily misinterpreted form. The Church received a lot of publicity because of that stand—and not necessarily positive publicity.

While at work one day I received a phone call from a woman

who was the director of the Mrs. Utah Pageant. She said she had heard I would be an excellent contender for the title. I immediately laughed aloud and said: "Thank you, but I don't enter pageants, I judge them. I would be happy to judge this pageant for you." She replied that she had enough judges already and was looking for qualified contestants. Again I told her I wouldn't be interested. But she requested that I go home and discuss it with my husband and said she would call me back the next day. I said, "Fine, but I'm sure the answer will be no."

When I got home from work that day I told my husband what had happened. As I was laughing about the whole idea I looked at Doug and was surprised to see he was not laughing. He said, "Do it." I couldn't believe my ears. Me, be in a beauty pageant? Doug said, "I think it will be an excellent growing experience for you, Vivian." So with gentle persuasion from friends and family and a major *push* from my husband I entered the pageant.

There were three areas of competition in this pageant: the personal interviews, which counted 50 percent; the formal competition, which counted 25 percent; and the swimwear competition, which accounted for the remaining 25 percent.

With a formal my husband had bought me just six months earlier and a borrowed swimsuit, lo and behold I actually won! I couldn't believe it! I had won the title of Mrs. Utah America.

You may have noticed that funny things happen sometimes to women who have crowns on their heads. I was no exception. Suddenly I was no longer Vivian Cline; I was now Queen Vivian. All of those twinkly stars in my crown went straight to my head.

After a blessing from my husband, off to the nationals I flew to fulfill my destiny and become Mrs. America. The nationals, however, were a different ball game from the Utah experience. I was now competing against forty-nine other winners who all had the same sparkle in their eyes.

Ten grueling days of competition followed. The hours of rehearsals and the pressures of competition were taxing. But my confidence waxed strong as I remembered that the Lord was behind me and would bless me with the strength I needed in meeting this schedule.

Through the week I felt as though I was doing really well in the preliminary judging. My formal was sure to pull points, because it was so different from the others. I was one of the few women there who was actually covered.

The final area of competition was the personal interview. This is where you either made it or lost it, because it counted 50 percent of the total points.

I clearly remember that day and how nervous I was. I couldn't even sit down. Pacing back and forth, I would watch the contestants who preceded me come out of the personal interview room. One of them came out with tears in her eyes, and I knew then that this part of the competition was going to be really tough.

Suddenly I heard the words that made my whole body shiver. "Mrs. Utah, please come in."

With a deep breath and my head held high, I placed a smile on my face and said: "Yes. Thank you."

Gracefully I entered a small room where a panel of six judges was seated. Directly in front of them was the contestant's chair, in which I was invited to sit.

To my surprise I felt more calm and comfortable than I had supposed I could be. My thoughts were clear, my words crisp. I answered questions regarding my career and the sole question they asked about my family. I felt totally at ease. The judges and I laughed together and even teased about some aspects of the beauty business.

All at once the national director said, "Time is up." Four minutes had gone fast. As I started to get up from my chair, I felt good and knew that I had done well.

Then it happened. A hand came straight up in front of me as one of the women judges said: "Excuse me for asking this question, Mrs. Utah, but you are from Utah. Are you a Mormon?"

(When I later related this story to one of my friends, she laughed and said, "You should have said to them, 'If I say yes, does that mean I have to bring the cookies and punch?' ")

I didn't pause or hesitate when the question was asked, but proudly responded, "Yes, I am."

The judge now asked, "Tell me, why is your church prejudiced against blacks?"

I was dumbfounded. I couldn't believe she had asked such a question. Quickly I told her that we were not prejudiced against blacks, that many members of the Church were black, and we had missions in Africa.

A famous fashion designer next followed suit. "Tell me why you kick kids out of Brigham Young University who have long hair and beards, and yet Brigham Young himself had long hair and a beard."

"That's an easy question to answer" I replied. "In Brigham Young's time it was very fashionable for men to have long hair and a beard. Even the most decent men had them."

"Are you saying that men with long hair and a beard are not decent?" he retorted.

"No," I said, "That's just the way you interpreted it."

It was beginning to get very warm in that room. Another judge now joined the attack with: "Do you really believe everything the Mormon church teaches? I mean, everything?"

Calmly I answered: "Yes, I do. One hundred percent."

Then the big question came. A famous motion picture producer demanded, "Why did you recently excommunicate a woman from your church just because she believes in ERA?"

This one I was really ready for. I had read all the Church publications on the Equal Rights Amendment and had stayed abreast of media reports on what was going on. I was well aware of the instance he referred to.

"The woman you mention was excommunicated not for her belief in ERA but for other reasons," I explained. "If a person is a member of your club and he doesn't support the president of your club nor the by-laws, you don't let him remain a member, now, do you?"

In a very heated and agitated manner the producer said, "I believe I'm the one asking the questions."

"No," I said, "you would not."

By this time the national director was about to have a cardiac arrest. We had been having an additional interview, and she knew that was totally improper. Hurriedly she said: "It's time to go. We must go now."

Again I began to rise from my chair. I stood tall, smiled, and made for the door. Then I heard one last question.

"Tell me, Mrs. Utah," the fiery producer asked, "do *you* believe in ERA?"

I couldn't believe my ears. The audacity this man had, questioning my integrity! He knew that only the panel of judges, the national director, and I were in that room. He knew that, like the other contestants, I wanted that national crown. It would have been so easy to tell him what he wanted to hear.

With my back straight and my head held high I looked into his face and said with a smile, "No."

He rolled his eyes up to the ceiling in disgust as I left the room.

Outside in the waiting area the other contestants ran up to me and asked me how it had gone. I smiled and calmly said: "It was great. You're going to love it. It was a breeze." Then I went back to my hotel room, called my mother long-distance . . . and cried my heart out.

I had just been raked over the coals because of my religious beliefs. It was almost more than I could bear.

The next morning the national director approached me at rehearsal and said, "Mrs. Utah, may I see you for a moment, please."

She then proceeded to walk away from the other contestants so we could have some privacy. She told me: "The judges came to me after the personal interview session yesterday and said that they had come down on you pretty hard. If you would like a formal apology from them they will be happy to give you one."

Quickly I told the director that my concern was that they judge me according to the way I had responded to the questions and not on my personal and religious views. She assured me that they would.

Wanting to believe her, I quietly added, "How do you think I did?"

Looking around to make sure no one was listening, she whispered, "Personally, darling, I think you did a ——— good job."

That was all I needed to know. Again I felt confident that all was well. The final event came the next evening. There the names of the ten finalists would be called out and the selection of the queen and the runners-up would be made.

Now, I had been in the beauty business for a number of years, and I knew what it took to be in the top ten. I was confident that I would be a top-ten contender, but what I really wanted was at least to be a runner-up, because runners-up receive cash prizes. Being in pageants can be very expensive, and I had given my husband's charge cards a heat rash before leaving home. If I placed as a runner-up I could at least make enough money to break even.

What an exciting evening! There I was, standing on-stage with forty-nine other contestants in front of a huge audience, with national television cameras all around. It was as though I was actually living out a childhood fantasy. I stood tall, smiling from ear to ear with that cheesy smile that all such contestants have. I was thinking about how surprised I should look when they called my name out among the top ten.

The announcer began calling out the names of the finalists. When he got to the third name, suddenly something whispered to me, "Vivian, keep your back straight and your head high, because your name will not be called."

I was stunned. Of course my name would be called! I deserved to be in the top ten. Even though my personal interview had been heated, at least they couldn't forget me.

Contestants number four, five, and six were called. I began to get a little nervous. Number seven and eight. I swallowed hard. Number nine. I took a deep breath. And contestant number ten . . . My name was not read. I believe that one of the most difficult things I have ever had to do in my life was to stand in front of national television with a smile on my face when my heart was at my feet.

How could this have happened? How could they have been so unfair? This just wasn't right. Yet the decision had been made. There was nothing I could do about it.

The curtain began to close on all the losers as the finalists stepped forward. As tears began to well up in my eyes, Mrs. Georgia came up to me. She hadn't spoken to me all week; in fact, she had completely ignored me every time I had tried to befriend her.

"Mrs. Utah," she said with tears in her eyes, "I just wanted you to know that you were on my top ten list."

Somehow that didn't make me feel any better. I wanted to say: "I was on *my* top ten list too, and where did it get me? Nowhere." But instead I squeaked out a simple, "Thank you."

Luckily for me, my dear sweet husband was there at the pageant to console and comfort me. I don't know what I would have done without him.

The next day we left for home. All those sparkles left my eyes and I went back to my normal routine of family, church, and work responsibilities.

Several weeks later I received a letter in the mail with the sender shown as The Church of Jesus Christ of Latter-day Saints. That was not an unusual occurrence, because I do a lot of presentations and I regularly receive letters of confirmation. This was a little different, however, in that above the sender address were three very small letters—the initials S. W. K.

My first thoughts were to wonder who could possibly be sending me a letter *sealed with a kiss*. I quickly reasoned that it was probably someone I had dated at BYU who was now a bishop or stake president and was teasing me. I laughed as I tore the letter open to reveal the mystery writer. The letter read:

Dear Sister Cline:

It has just come to my attention that you won the Mrs. Utah Pageant contest in 1980, and that you competed with contestants from the other forty-nine states for the Mrs. America Pageant, held in Las Vegas, Nevada. We commend you for this honorable recognition. Congratulations!

I have also learned of the answers you gave to the questions asked by a panel of judges in Las Vegas while conducting the personal interview aspect of the contest. We are proud of you for your shining example, and for your loyalty and devotion to the Church. May the Lord bless you in all of your righteous endeavors.

Please be assured of my love and blessings, which I extend to you, and to your husband and family, with my kindest wishes.

Faithfully Yours,

Spencer W. Kimball

My dear young friends, I may have left a pageant in Las Vegas, Nevada, without a crown, but that experience and the rewards that resulted will far outlast a few cheap rhinestones. For you see, I am resolved that I *will* have the moral courage to make my actions consistent with my knowledge of right and wrong.

I urge you to join me in this resolution: We *will* "stand as witnesses of God at all times and in all things, and in all places" — and at *all* costs.

Vivian R. Cline, an owner of a finishing school in Salt Lake City and director of the "Polish with Pleasure" workshop at BYU, was Mrs. Utah-America in 1980. She likes traveling, working with youth, playing softball, and reading the scriptures. She appreciates the "receptiveness and honesty" of young people. Vivian and her husband, Douglas, have five children.